Sourdough Breads
from the Bread Machine

100 Surefire Recipes for Everyday Loaves, Artisan Breads, Baguettes, Bagels, Rolls, and More

MICHELLE ANDERSON

HARVARD COMMON PRESS

Inspiring | Educating | Creating | Entertaining

Brimming with creative inspiration, how-to projects, and useful information to enrich your everyday life, quarto.com is a favorite destination for those pursuing their interests and passions.

© 2022 Quarto Publishing Group USA Inc.
Text © 2022 Michelle Anderson
Photography © 2022 <if required>

First Published in 2022 by The Harvard Common Press, an imprint of The Quarto Group, 100 Cummings Center, Suite 265-D, Beverly, MA 01915, USA.
T (978) 282-9590 F (978) 283-2742 Quarto.com

The Harvard Common Press titles are also available at discount for retail, wholesale, promotional, and bulk purchase. For details, contact the Special Sales Manager by email at specialsales@quarto.com or by mail at The Quarto Group, Attn: Special Sales Manager, 100 Cummings Center, Suite 265-D, Beverly, MA 01915, USA.

26 25 24 23 22   1 2 3 4 5

ISBN: 978-0-7603-7474-0

Digital edition published in 2022

eISBN: 978-0-7603-7475-7

Library of Congress Cataloging-in-Publication Data

Anderson, Michelle (Chef), author.
Sourdough breads from the bread machine : 100 surefire recipes for
   everyday loaves, artisan breads, baguettes, bagels, rolls, and more /
   Michelle Anderson.
LCCN 2022005652 (print) | LCCN 2022005653 (ebook) | ISBN
   9780760374740 (trade paperback) | ISBN 9780760374757 (ebook)
1. Sourdough bread. 2. Cooking (Bread). 3. Automatic bread machines. 4. Cookbooks.
LCC TX770.S66 A53 2022 (print) | LCC TX770.S66 (ebook) |
   DDC 641.81/5--dc23/eng/20220214

Design: Laura Klynstra
Cover Image: Nicole Soper
Page Layout: Laura Klynstra
Photography: Nicole Soper; except for Shutterstock images on pages 23, 27, and 90

Printed in China

To Scott, Mac, and Coop,
as always.

Contents

Getting Started

I had nearly ten years of breadmaking under my belt before attempting a sourdough starter, and I was unsuccessful due to a relentless horde of fruit flies. Yuck. My next attempt fared better, and I named it Beatrice. Bea came with me to my next job and lived ten years in my kitchens until an apprentice forgot to remove her from an oven—where she was stored before firing it up. Tragedy.

After losing my starter Bea, I continued to make regular bread for my job, turning out heaps of golden loaves and tender buns for our clientele. I never really baked bread at home, and I certainly didn't nurture a starter in my already crowded kitchen. Perhaps I was too tired to make an effort with two young boys to raise and not enough hours in the day for all that kneading and proofing. So when my mother-in-law Diane gave me a bread machine as a gift, I was thrilled to find that five minutes of effort layering ingredients into the bucket was all I needed to create lovely, fragrant bread at home. That machine delighted me, and I recommended one to pretty much everyone I knew, even my culinary-challenged sister, since the device required no supervision or cooking knowledge.

When my boys moved out—Hallelujah, no empty nest syndrome here—I tried my hand at a white flour starter again. The process was easier than I remembered, and soon a lovely culture was bubbling happily next to my coffee machine on the counter. My husband was vaguely repulsed by the yeasty odor until I made a glorious, golden loaf in my bread machine using Fred (my starter). I felt fabulous combining my passion for sourdough with my beloved bread machine, and this book came about to share that satisfying pairing with you. This book will introduce you to the incredible world of sourdough bread and show you how to make it in your bread machine. There is a step-by-step walk-through of the science of sourdough starters, along with three recipes to make your own. You will learn about the ingredients used in breadmaking and how a bread machine works. I've also included a detailed troubleshooting section with handy information about fixing any issues. The recipe chapters contain a selection of bread, ranging from Soft Sourdough Sandwich Bread (page 57) to spectacular sweet bread such as Chocolate Cinnamon Bread (page 122). There are also two recipes finished in your oven. And there are recipes that use up the starter discard. So, let's make some bread!

Opposite: A nice and bubbly sourdough starter

PART ONE

All About Sourdough and Your Bread Machine

So, let's get started! This section might seem less fun than actual recipes, but being familiar with your bread machine and understanding sourdough is essential. This knowledge will help you create lovely, consistent loaves.

CHAPTER ONE

Getting to Know Sourdough

I have been baking for close to forty-five years, from when I made brownies in my Easy-Bake Oven to the glorious golden loaf of bread that I took out of my bread machine today. And there is nothing quite like the scent of fresh bread. That yeasty, slightly sweet fragrance wraps around you like a warm summer breeze. Sourdough bread is even better; its tanginess adds a delightful layer of complexity. Sourdough is intimidating until you create your own, and it's completely worth every minute of effort. So, let's learn about sourdough and get started.

What Is Sourdough Bread?

Sourdough bread has been around for centuries, from around 1500 BCE in Egypt, although it was not called sourdough. People kept a live culture of wild yeast in a liquid medium—a starter—in their home to create the bread that was often the base of a filling meal. You couldn't just run to the grocery store to pick up baker's yeast back then; it took a wee bit more effort. These starters were passed from family to friends to family for generations and could live for a very long time. For example, the one living in my refrigerator currently comes from an 1849 starter carried by Basque gold miners in San Francisco.

Until baker's yeast—a fast-growing strain called *Saccharomyces cerevisiae*—showed up in the 1970s in small packets, sourdough was the method used to create leavened bread. Using commercial yeast is convenient, but being part of rich history and utilizing ancient techniques when producing your own bread is satisfying.

Sourdough bread depends on a starter—a combination of flour, water, wild yeast, and *lactobacilli* (a healthy bacteria found in flour) to leaven it, rather than baker's yeast. The *lactobacilli* create lactic acid, and the combination of this lactic acid and the alcohol produced by the yeast produces the signature tangy sourdough flavor. You might already be familiar with *lactobacilli* bacteria if you are a fan of fermented foods such as sauerkraut, kefir, and pickles.

Can You Make Sourdough Bread in a Machine?

This question is one I often get from family and friends interested in trying sourdough baking. So, can you make sourdough bread using a bread machine? The answer is yes, and no. As defined by aficionados, traditional sourdough bread needs a slow rise, often 12 to 24 hours, which is not possible with basic bread machine settings. Plus, these settings have set kneading, rise, punching down, and baking times that might not suit some sourdough recipes.

Most people are interested in sourdough because of the many benefits (page 18) of using a starter and the lovely flavor sourdough produces in bread and other recipes. Although bread machines are not specifically designed to deal with the unique needs of sourdough bread, you can still create tasty, beautiful loaves with a few tweaks. You will need to make an active sourdough starter for the recipes in this book—never fear—but the bread machine process will be slightly different from the traditional method.

There are two ways to use your bread machine for sourdough; I have used both with great success. The recipes in this book use the simplest tweak: added yeast with the starter and other ingredients to accelerate the rise. This is an acceptable practice in France, where bakers can add a specific percentage of extra yeast to their sourdough. The amount of yeast can vary depending on the strength of your starter, so you might have to experiment initially. You can remove the paddle(s) from the bucket after the kneading cycle is complete if your starter is strong because sourdough does not need to be punched down. Then the program will run until the end.

The second method is closer to the standard sourdough breadmaking practice and is excellent when you have extra time to bake your bread. You will omit the extra yeast and run the bread machine on the dough function. When the kneading cycle is complete and the dough is a nice uniform ball, unplug the machine, remove the paddles, and let the dough rise naturally for 8 to 12 hours. I like to do this overnight. When the dough has risen, plug the machine back in, and run the Bake (or Bake Now) program.

Using the second method, your loaf will have a more robust sourdough flavor, but either produces delicious bread with very little supervision or work. The recipes in chapter 8 that are formed and baked outside the bread machine use a combination of these techniques.

The Sourdough Process . . . Simplified

You might be familiar with yeast, perhaps made bread for decades, but have never attempted sourdough before now. A sourdough starter is different from regular yeast; it is alive and requires feeding. Let's look at the process of creating a sourdough starter to understand how it works and how to keep yours healthy. You don't need much to make a starter: flour, water, a container with a lid, plastic wrap, a cloth, measuring cups, and a spoon. And the wild yeast found all around you (see page 16).

Depending on the amount of starter you want to make, add a measure of flour—1 or 2 cups (125 to 250 g)—and half that amount of water. Stir it to create a paste. The flour enzymes split the starches into sugars, which are then fed on by yeast (present everywhere) and *lactobacilli* bacteria. Just loosely cover the container with plastic wrap or a cloth and leave the container at room temperature to let this feeding frenzy happen.

After 24 hours, you will remove half and discard it. Add back 1 cup (125 g) of flour and ½ cup (120 ml) of water. The starter will get frothy and bubbly. This process will continue for 3 or 4 days as microorganisms form acids, ethanol, and carbon dioxide as they consume the sugars. At the same time, *lactobacilli* change sugars to acetic and lactic acid, souring the starter and dropping the pH to around 3.8. This acidic environment is too much for the microorganisms except for acid-tolerating wild yeast, which creates carbon dioxide and ethanol out of the sugars.

After about 5 days, the starter is an actual science project; it ferments vigorously and smells quite distinctive. You might notice a liquid floating on the surface known as hooch; just stir it back into the starter. If you keep discarding half and feeding the remainder, it will continue to thrive. If leaving the starter out at room temperature, discard/feed it every day and if in the refrigerator, discard/feed it once a week. Think about the fact that each teaspoon of sourdough starter contains five billion *lactobacilli* and fifty million yeasts.

To determine whether your starter is ready, fill a glass with warm water and drop a teaspoon of the starter into it. If the starter floats, it has enough air bubbles and is ready. If it sinks, keep feeding it at room temperature. To slow down the yeast growth, store the sourdough starter in the refrigerator and feed it once a week or when you want to bake bread.

Benefits of Eating Sourdough

Sourdough bread offers some wonderful benefits besides the incredible taste—which is more than enough reason to eat it.

- **Source of prebiotics:** Sourdough starter is packed with living "good" bacteria. The prebiotics in the starter survive the heat of baking and provide food for the bacteria in the gut. This leads to an improved digestive system and boosts your immunity.

- **Easy to digest:** The bacterium in the starter predigests the flour in the dough while the dough rises, and voilà! It's easier to digest, even for those who have gluten sensitivity.

- **Increases bioavailability of nutrients:** Grains do not break down well because they contain antinutrients—such as gluten and phytic acid—which block the absorption of nutrients. The bacteria in sourdough starter breaks down the phytic acid so the body can absorb the nutrients in the bread.

- **Helps manage blood sugar:** During fermentation, the starches and sugars in the flour are eaten by the yeast, so sourdough bread ends up lower on the glycemic index. This means your blood sugar will not spike very much when you eat a slice.

- **More "good acid":** Sourdough bread contains more *lactobacilli*, resulting in higher levels of lactic acid. This leaves less space for potentially unhealthy phytic acid. More lactic acid increases the availability of minerals and supports easier digestion.

- **Nutritious:** Sourdough bread isn't health food, but it contains moderate or small amounts of vitamins and nutrients, including B vitamins, calcium, folate, iron, magnesium, manganese, niacin, phosphorus, potassium, riboflavin, selenium, thiamin, vitamin E, and zinc.

Sourdough Starter Recipes

I make my own starters for bread—these are my go-to recipes—but I also, on occasion, use an internet-purchased starter that is quicker and is quite foolproof. My favorite comes from Kensington Market in Toronto, Ontario, from an original San Francisco sourdough starter. No matter how you get your starter going is fine.

WHITE/WHOLE WHEAT/ RYE STARTER

This is the traditional method of making a starter—gathering the wild yeast from the air. For some reason, it is strangely exciting to see this one start to bubble, almost like magic!

Prep time: 10 minutes, plus fermenting time

1 cup (125 g) all-purpose/ whole wheat/rye flour

½ cup (120 ml) filtered or bottled water

Day 1: In a glass bowl or container, combine the flour and water with a wooden spoon until well combined. Loosely cover the bowl with plastic wrap or partially cover with a lid. Set it aside in a warm spot for 24 hours.

Day 2: Discard half the starter and stir in 1 cup (125 g) of flour and ½ cup (120 ml) of warm water. Cover it up again and set it aside for 24 hours at room temperature.

Day 3 to Day 7: Transfer ½ cup (113 g) starter to a clean glass jar or bowl (discard the remainder, it is unusable at this point) and stir in 1 cup (125 g) of flour and ½ cup (120 ml) of warm water. Cover and set aside for 24 hours at room temperature. You will notice bubbles, and the starter will smell sour.

Cover the starter and place it in the refrigerator. Feed it every week by removing all but ½ cup (113 g) or so of the starter and adding back 1 cup (125 g) of flour and ½ cup (120 ml) of warm water. (Use the discard in a tasty recipe, page 185.) Let the starter sit out for a few hours until doubled and then store, covered, back in the refrigerator.

When you need a starter for a recipe—for example, 1 cup (225– 235 g) active, fed starter—transfer ½ tablespoon (7 g) of starter to a jar and stir in 1 cup (125 g) of flour and ½ cup (120 ml) of water and let stand at room temperature until doubled and spongy. Stir any remaining starter back into your main container.

If you bake every day or several times a week, you can store the starter at room temperature, partially covered. Feed the starter once a day by removing all but ½ cup (113 g) of starter (use in a recipe, page 185, or discard). Stir in ½ cup (113 g) of flour and ½ cup (120 ml) of water.

GLUTEN-FREE SOURDOUGH STARTER

I didn't know for years that gluten-free starters were even possible. This is a wonderful way to enjoy sourdough baking and still follow your diet.

Prep time: 10 minutes, plus fermenting time

¼ cup (37 g) 1:1 gluten-free flour blend

¼ cup (30 g) brown rice or buckwheat flour

½ cup (120 ml) filtered or bottled water

1:1 gluten-free flour, for feeding

Day 1: Stir together the flour blend, brown rice or buckwheat flour, and water in a glass bowl or 4-cup (940-ml) jar until a thick paste forms. Cover the top loosely with plastic wrap. Set it aside in a warm spot for 24 hours.

Day 2: Transfer ¼ cup (56–59 g) of the mixture to a clean bowl (discard the remainder in the bowl). Stir in ¼ cup (37 g) gluten-free flour blend, ¼ cup (30 g) brown rice flour, and ½ cup (120 ml) water. Cover and set aside for 24 hours at room temperature.

Day 3 to Day 7: Repeat this process (transfer, discard, and feed) for the next 5 days. You will notice bubbles and the starter rising and falling. When the starter falls, feed it.

After 7 Days: Transfer the starter to a clean container, refrigerate, and continue to feed it as required. Feed the starter by transferring ½ cup (112–118 g) to a clean jar or bowl (use the remaining starter for a discard recipe, page 185). Stir in ⅔ cup (160 ml) of water and ⅔ cup (99 g) 1:1 gluten-free or brown rice flour. Cover, and set it aside to double—this could take from 4 to 8 hours—and scoop out what is needed for the recipe.

Store the remaining starter covered in the refrigerator. If you are not baking very often, feed your starter once a week.

SOURDOUGH STARTER WITH YEAST

This is a never-fail starter recipe that is not dependent on gathering wild yeast. It is ready faster, so you can start baking sooner!

Prep time: 10 minutes, plus fermenting time

1 cup (125 g) all-purpose flour or whole wheat flour

1⅛ teaspoons active dry yeast

1 cup (240 ml) warm water (100°F to 110°F, or 38°C to 43°C)

Stir the flour and yeast in a large glass bowl. Slowly whisk in the water until the mixture is smooth. Cover the bowl with a clean kitchen cloth and let stand at room temperature until it smells sour and is bubbly, between 2 and 4 days.

Transfer the starter to a clean mason jar or glass bowl. Store it covered in the refrigerator until you wish to use it.

Feed the starter once a week by discarding all but ½ cup (use the discard in a recipe, page 185). Feed the remainder with 1 cup (125 g) of flour and ½ cup (120 ml) of warm water.

When you wish to activate the starter for a recipe, scoop out ½ cup (120 ml), feed with ½ cup (120 ml) of water and 1 cup (125 g) of flour. Let stand at room temperature until doubled and bubbly, about 8 to 10 hours.

FREEZING YOUR BACKUP STARTER

Sourdough starters can be frozen to keep as a backup. Pour the extra starter in ice cube trays and freeze until solid. Remove the cubes from the tray and transfer them to a sealed plastic bag for up to a year. When you want to use the starter, transfer two cubes (¼ cup) to a glass bowl or jar and let it thaw. Add ½ cup (113 g) of flour and ¼ cup (60 ml) of warm water, and stir until combined. Let stand at room temperature until it has doubled, and then store or use.

Bread Ingredients
FLOUR

Flour—some type—is in all bread. Wheat flour is the traditional choice because it contains gluten-forming proteins such as gliadin (adds adhesive properties to the gluten) and glutenin (adds elasticity and strength to the gluten). When you add liquid to flour, hydrating the proteins, long strands of gluten form to produce the structure of the bread. To make this foundation more complex and more substantial, the dough needs to be stretched and kneaded. The carbon dioxide bubbles produced by the yeast are trapped in this structure, causing the dough to rise, and the natural sugar in the flour feeds the yeast.

The types of wheat flour include:

- **All-purpose flour:** All-purpose flour is milled to remove the wheat germ and bran, so it is fluffy and light. USA all-purpose flour is made from hard and soft wheat, and its gluten content is between 9 and 11 percent. Canadian all-purpose flour is 100 percent hard wheat, so it has 11 to 14 percent gluten content. This is comparable to bread flour from other regions in the world. You can get either bleached or unbleached all-purpose flour. Unbleached flour is aged, which lightens the color and oxidizes the protein. Bleached flour is less nutritious, so you will often see enriched products with calcium, iron, and B vitamins added back in.

- **Bread flour:** Bread flour is used in bread recipes because its higher protein—11 to 14 percent—creates an elastic dough and springy bread. If you substitute bread flour for all-purpose flour in a recipe, add a tablespoon (15 ml) of liquid per cup of flour.

- **White whole wheat flour:** This flour is milled from a higher protein variety—white spring wheat—and has 12 percent protein.

- **Whole wheat flour:** 100 percent whole wheat flour contains the entire wheat berry. It comes in fine and coarse ground and has a lovely nutty flavor. Whole wheat flour is about 16 percent protein, and it produces a chewy, denser loaf. Despite its higher protein content, whole wheat loaves need longer to rise because the hull in the flour cuts the gluten strands.

- **Gluten-free flours:** You can make gluten-free sourdough bread, there is a starter on page 20, but none of the recipes in this book are gluten-free. If you want to convert them, try a 1:1 gluten-free flour blend and experiment until you are happy with the results. The various gluten-free flours taste different, so the flavor of your bread will change depending on the blend. Some of the most commonly used gluten-free flours include:

  - *Almond flour:* This is a coarser flour that creates a tender, sometimes crumbly bread.

  - *Amaranth flour:* This is a high protein and fiber flour that absorbs liquid, so it produces a dense bread.

- *Arrowroot:* Powdery and flavorless, this flour can lighten bread texture but is not used in large quantities in blends.

- *Bean flours:* These assertive tasting, high protein flours are best used in bread such as pumpernickel or anything with cocoa powder.

- *Brown rice flour:* This sandy-textured, nutty-tasting flour is high in fiber, protein, fat, and other nutrients. It works well in most bread recipes.

- *Buckwheat:* This flour has a distinctive, pleasant flavor and is popular in blends.

- *Cassava flour:* The texture and taste is very similar to all-purpose wheat flour. It's a good choice for a blend.

- *Chickpea flour:* This is a dense, strong-tasting flour that is suited to flatbreads.

- *Coconut flour:* This is a pleasant coconut-tasting flour. Keep in mind that it is extremely absorbent and should be no more than 25 percent of a blend or the bread will fall apart.

- *Millet flour:* This coarse, nutty-tasting flour should be used in moderation if you want a finer textured bread. It is higher in structure-creating protein than many other gluten-free choices, but can leave a chalky taste.

- *Potato starch:* This is an excellent binder, so it is often included in gluten-free flour blends. It has a neutral taste, too.

- *Sorghum flour:* The flavor of this flour is very similar to wheat flour, so it is an excellent choice for bread.

- *Teff flour:* This neutral-tasting, high protein flour is often found in blends.

WHAT IS GLUTEN?

Gluten is the protein in cereal grains that creates bread's structure, producing a springy loaf rather than the dense crumb of a cake or crumbly cookie texture. When two proteins—glutenin and gliadin—in cereal grains mix with water, they bind together into chains. When the dough is kneaded, the chains multiply and elongate, creating the gluten network responsible for the structure of bread. The longer the dough is kneaded, the more intricate and stronger the gluten network becomes, and when you fold the dough, the gluten strands line up, and the webbing can trap the carbon dioxide gas produced by the yeast more effectively. Kneading the dough with a machine rather than by hand hydrates the dough better, so gluten can form quickly.

Factors that influence gluten development are the essential ingredients used in breadmaking:

- **Flour:** The higher the protein, the more gluten: 11 percent to 13 percent is best. Some cereal grains—such as rye—need to be blended with whole wheat because they do not contain sufficient protein.

- **Water amount:** Too little or too much water will inhibit the creation of the gluten network.

- **Dairy:** Too much milk can kill the gluten because it is high in enzymes, so you need to scald these ingredients to approximately 212°F (100°C) to destroy them.

- **Fat:** Fat blocks hydration by coating the proteins. This means the proteins don't bind together, and the strands stay short, so the bread takes longer to rise.

- **Salt:** The chlorine in salt strengthens the gluten network because this chemical element helps gluten proteins stick together.

- **Sugar:** Too much sugar will block proteins from binding effectively because the sugar competes with the protein by attaching to the water molecules instead.

WATER

Bread is mostly water—between 60 and 85 percent—and the higher the percentage, the more holes in the bread: think ciabatta. Water is needed to activate the yeast, disperse the yeast throughout the dough, form the gluten, moisten the dough, and dissolve other ingredients. Do not use hard water, if possible, because the magnesium sulfate in this water will retard yeast action, which impedes the rise. Also, yeast thrives in an acidic environment, and hard water tends to be alkaline. If you live in an area with hard water, stick to distilled or bottled water for making bread.

YEAST

Yeast is a living ingredient; there are millions of these single-cell organisms in a single teaspoon. These organisms give bread its signature smell and taste. When you activate yeast with water, yeast releases an enzyme that changes whatever sugar is present into dextrose. Carbon dioxide is released when this dextrose breaks down, and this gas is trapped in the gluten strands, creating the coveted rise. This gas expands further when you bake bread, and you get a lovely light and airy texture.

This book uses sourdough starter (page 19) and bread machine yeast, but there are other kinds you can try if breadmaking becomes a passion. Yeast products are not interchangeable, so stick to whatever is called for in the recipe. Store your yeast in the refrigerator or freezer to keep it fresh, and don't use it past its expiry date, or your bread will not rise. Take the time to keep all combined liquids between 100°F and 110°F (38°C and 43°C) for optimal yeast activity; you don't want to kill it in a hot temperature or create sluggish yeast if too cold.

- **Cake or compressed yeast:** This highly perishable, living yeast needs to be stored in the refrigerator, and it produces more carbon dioxide than the other types. It will last about 2 weeks.

- **Active dry yeast:** Many regular recipes (outside a bread machine) use this dehydrated yeast. It is inert until proofed with water and sometimes a little sugar.

- **Rapid rise yeast or bread machine yeast:** These granules are small and inert but do not need proofing.

- **Instant dry yeast:** You can use this in a bread machine; the yeast is milled into finer granules than active dry yeast. The rise is speedy, and you can add this type directly to the dry ingredients; no proofing is required.

SALT

Few bread recipes omit the salt because this ingredient serves many purposes in the process; even sweet breads have a dash or two. It should be no surprise that salt adds flavor, but it also strengthens and stabilizes the gluten network and slows yeast fermentation, so your bread doesn't collapse from rising too fast and high. Salt must be added to the liquid ingredients and kept away from the yeast because salt can kill it. Fine salt is best for the dough, but flaky coarse salt is a lovely finish sprinkled on the surface just before baking.

FATS AND OILS

There is a broad range of fats and oils that you can try, such as olive oil, bacon fat, shortening, butter, vegetable oil, nut oils, or margarine. Fat plays several roles in breadmaking. The lubrication allows the other ingredients to slide, which improves the rise; however, the more fat you use, the longer the rise takes because fat coats the yeast. This slows the formation of carbon dioxide, so bread like brioche with heaps of added butter needs more time. Fats create a lovely fluffy texture, greater volume, and depending on the type used, enhance flavor, as well.

SUGAR

This ingredient serves several purposes in the breadmaking process. As expected, it adds sweetness to the interior and color to the crust through caramelization. Sugar is also consumed by yeast, which then produces carbon dioxide and alcohol, creating the desired rise. Flour contains sugar—about 2 to 3 percent—but this amount is not enough to feed the yeast. You need to add extra in the form of granulated sugar, honey, brown sugar, maple syrup, or molasses, under ¼ cup in most cases. Since sugar attaches to water molecules, if more than ¼ cup is used, the added sugar will compete with the proteins in the flour for water, and gluten formation will be impeded. This competition is the reason sweet breads take longer to rise—more sugar in the dough. If you prefer using a liquid form of sugar, such as maple syrup or honey, instead of granulated, remember to count it as a liquid and remove an equal amount from the water or milk in the recipe.

EGGS

Eggs are most common in sweet bread because they add fat, protein, richness, flavor, and color to the recipe. Lovely tender challah and brioche highlight the benefit of adding eggs. Extra fat is added to recipes that include eggs because their extra protein can tighten the gluten, so fat counters that effect. Eggs are part of the liquid in bread, so if you omit them, add ¼ cup (60 ml) of another liquid to make up the difference.

DAIRY

This component includes milk—the second most popular liquid used in bread recipes—sour cream, yogurt, buttermilk, various cheeses, and butter. Milk creates a tender bread and lovely golden crust due to milk sugar caramelizing while baking. Butter is considered fat in bread recipes, and sour cream, yogurt, and buttermilk fall in the liquid category. Cheeses can be added to the dough or sprinkled on top, depending on your preference.

EXTRA INGREDIENTS

Bread flavor and texture can be enhanced by many ingredients besides the basics. You just have to be careful about the amount you throw in because too much can impede yeast action, or the loaf could end up unpleasantly dense.

Here are some extras to consider adding to your bread:

- **Chocolate:** One of my favorites! This ingredient can be added as cocoa powder (pumpernickel) or solid chocolate (chocolate babka). Cocoa powder adds color and can be bitter or sweet, depending on the sugar amount in the recipe. All types of solid can be used, from white to deep dark chocolate, as chips, chunks, or grated.

- **Citrus:** Zest—fresh or candied—adds intense flavor to bread-like panettone. Fresh is added along with the flour and larger candied chunks when the machine signals to add extras.

- **Coconut:** Coconut (sweetened or unsweetened) adds flavor and texture to the bread. Use grated, shredded, or flaked. Add it in with the flour.

- **Coffee:** Coffee creates complex flavor in rye or black bread, added as a powder or liquid. If using fresh-brewed, make sure it cools to the correct temperature to not kill the yeast.

- **Fruit:** Purées, fresh fruit, and dried fruit add flavor, texture, and color to the bread. Add purées to the liquid ingredients. If adding fresh fruit, cut it in tiny chunks and add a little extra flour to offset the juice. Dried is added when the machine signals.

- **Herbs:** This is a very popular additive to bread; fresh and dried add incredible flavor. Try basil, oregano, thyme, rosemary, dill, or chives.

- **Nuts:** Many bread recipes use nuts for flavor and texture. They are added when the machine signals if chopped, or along with the flour. Make sure the amount of chopped nuts is under 1 cup (weight varies) or the bread might not rise. Try almonds, cashews, hazelnuts, pine nuts, pecans, pistachios, and walnuts.

- **Seeds:** This is a favorite of mine—sesame, sunflower, pumpkin, chia, poppy, caraway, flaxseed, and fennel—find their way into many recipes. Add them along with the flour or scatter them on top.

- **Skim milk powder:** This ingredient creates a lovely, tender crumb and golden crust. I often add a couple tablespoons (16 g) along with the flour.

- **Spices:** Sweet and savory bread benefits from spices such as anise, cinnamon, nutmeg, cumin, cloves, cardamom, and black pepper. Use spices in small amounts because the flavor is potent and can overwhelm the bread.

- **Vegetables:** Grated or puréed veggies enhance bread with flavor, texture, and color. Add them to the liquid ingredients. Try beets, carrots, zucchini, potatoes, sweet potato, and garlic.

- **Whole grains:** This is different from whole grain flour. Oats, bulgur, quinoa, farro, and wheat berries boost nutrition, flavor, and texture. Some are added cooked, so follow the recipe directions.

ADDING CHEESE TO BREAD

Yes, cheese deserves its own section because adding it to bread is delicious, but it needs to be handled carefully. Cheese can be added right to the dough or sprinkled on top.

When adding cheese:

- Cheese should be at room temperature.

- If using a salty cheese—feta, Roquefort, pecorino Romano—reduce the salt in the recipe

- Hard cheese—Parmigiano-Reggiano, Grana Padano, Vintage Gouda—should be used in small amounts. Grate or cut into small cubes (¼ inch, or 6 mm) because it will not melt as the bread is baking.

- Soft or semi-firm cheese—Cheddar, mozzarella, Havarti—can be cubed (½ to ¼ inch, or 1 to ½ cm) or grated.

- Creamy/soft cheeses—cream cheese, mascarpone, ricotta—can be added while the dough is kneaded to blend it in.

Always follow the recipe directions when adding cheese; it is often considered a liquid unless sprinkled on top. Too much can impede yeast activity, or the bread can be greasy.

If after you add the cheese, the dough looks too sticky and wet, add flour by the tablespoon until it looks right.

CHAPTER TWO

Making Sourdough Using a Bread Machine

Whether you are a sourdough veteran who wants to try making these lovely loaves in a bread machine, a bread machine expert trying your hand at sourdough, or a newbie to both, this section will give you all the information you need.

Five Reasons to Bake Sourdough Bread in a Machine

The scent of baking bread is like nothing in the world; it embraces you like a hug when you enter the house. You can undoubtedly make bread old-school with your own hands—from start to finish—but why not get similar, if not the same, results using a bread machine?

Here are just a few benefits of using a bread machine to make sourdough bread:

- **Energy-efficient:** A bread machine costs less to run than a standard oven, between 0.36–0.41 kilowatt-hour (kWh).

- **Set it and forget it:** There is no supervision needed for a bread machine; you layer in the ingredients, press Start, and walk away. You can even set some machines to start while you're at work or sleeping, so the loaf is ready after a long day or when you wake up.

- **Easy clean-up:** All the mixing, kneading, and baking are done in the machine, so clean-up is quick and effortless. All you need to wash is the bucket, paddles, and a couple measuring tools.

- **Convenience:** Baking will not take up valuable oven space if you want a loaf to serve with a meal. No juggling or time management is required! If you want to add nuts, dried fruit, or cheese, most machines will signal to remind you, and some will automatically feed the ingredients into the dough.

- **Simple for beginners:** Bread machines allow new bread bakers to produce perfect loaves the first time they try a recipe. No wasted time, ingredients, and disappointment here!

Which Is the Best Bread Machine for You?

When meandering down the bread machine aisle at a local store or researching brands online, you will notice a broad range of machines available. Although there are standard functions across all types, it can be overwhelming to choose the one that suits your needs.

This section will outline factors to consider, and describe the bells and whistles available:

- **Budget:** This is the most crucial consideration. Bread machine prices range from $60 to more than $300, so most people can find a device. Lower-end models produce lovely loaves, whereas pricier machines often have more settings and options. Pick a comfortable price point and look at what is available there.

- **Size:** Most machines offer more than one size—this book requires a 2-pound loaf capacity. If you are making bread for only yourself or two people, you probably don't need a 3-pound option because homemade bread has no preservatives. Also, consider the amount of counter space or storage space you have available. If it's limited, consider a smaller machine.

- **Bucket and paddles:** Original bread machines created tall vertical loaves and had one paddle to do the work. To create loaves that appeared oven-baked, manufacturers put out horizontal buckets with two paddles. The latter loaves serve easier in traditional-size slices, but the paddles do not knead well, so you often get flour in the corners. The machines with the rectangular buckets are larger, so again, consider space. I like removable buckets for easier cleaning and removable paddles, so you don't have to bake them into the bread.

- **Programs:** What do you want to bake? Most machines have Basic, Whole Wheat, Sweet, French, Dough, and Express Bake functions—all you need for recipes in this book. Additional programs are great, but if you don't need to make gluten-free bread or bake a cake in the machine, don't pay extra for them. Convenient settings are a delayed or timed start, especially if you want your loaf ready at a particular time and crust color from light to dark.

- **Alarm or ingredient dispenser:** If you like bread with lots of extras, invest in a machine that has an alarm for when to add dried fruit, cheese, nuts, and other ingredients. This feature is not essential if you don't mind timing the kneading cycle, but it is handy. If you don't want to add extras, look for a device with an automatic dispenser. You just put the ingredients in the drawer, and the machine adds them at the correct time.

Bread Machine Cycles

The preprogrammed cycles of bread machines are what provide the convenience of these handy devices. Different machines offer a range of cycles—usually more for a higher price—but even the most budget-friendly model has the ones needed for the recipes in this book.

Generally, most bread machines offer the following ten cycles:

- **Basic/White Bread:** I use this the most because it is flexible. The cycle will vary with browning and loaf size, but you can expect it to take 3 to 4 hours. Try it for recipes that use white flour or ones with up to 25 percent whole wheat, oat, or rye.

- **Delay or Timed Bake:** For recipes that do not include perishables such as milk, eggs, or butter. You place the ingredients in the bucket and set exactly when you want the machine to start the cycle.

- **Dough:** This takes the labor of kneading out of your hands—literally—and handles the first rise, as well. When the cycle is done, you remove the dough from the bucket, shape, rise again, and bake the loaf/buns/loaves in the oven.

- **French:** For crusty, hard-crusted loaves inspired by French and Italian bread. You will notice the cycle is longer because the rise is longer.

- **Gluten-Free:** This is a shorter cycle because gluten-free bread does not rise like regular bread.

- **Quick Bread:** If you make non-yeast bread, this is the cycle for you. The timing is shorter, just mixing and baking, and the lift in the bread is created with baking soda and baking powder.

- **Rapid/Quick/Express Bake:** You probably won't use this for sourdough bread, but you can produce a pretty decent loaf in under 1 hour using the rapid bake setting. This is achieved by a hefty addition of yeast (2 tablespoons [24 g] in some recipes) and shortened rise time.

- **Sweet:** If the recipe includes high amounts of sugar, fat, or eggs, you will be setting the machine to "Sweet." It has a lower baking temperature to ensure the crust doesn't burn.

- **Whole Wheat/Whole Grain:** The kneading and rising time are longer to accommodate the whole wheat or whole grain flours. If you need a whole wheat loaf quicker, add some vital wheat gluten and use the Basic/White cycle.

- **Bake:** You might want to try this for sourdough bread because it is basically like baking in the oven. If you want a "natural rise with no added yeast," set the bread dough in the bread maker, let the loaf rise overnight, and then bake.

TEMPERATURE IN BREADMAKING

When I started making bread in the 1980s, I did not use a thermometer for either ingredient temps or finished loaves; frankly, I was lucky when the oven temperature was within 100°F (38°C) of what I set. I continued throwing temperature caution to the wild until my last few years working in a professional kitchen. I always carried a sanitized instant digital thermometer in my chef coat pocket and one day casually inserted it into one of the many baking loaves after doing the thump—my tried-and-true bread readiness test—and got a 192°F (89°C) reading. Hmmm, interesting. So I kept trying, and eventually, rather than burn my fingers thumping, I did a quick read and never looked back. You do not have to utilize a thermometer to check doneness, but it is essential for measuring ingredients.

Yeast is most active between 100°F and 110°F (38°C and 43°C), so take the time to measure the liquid ingredients, including eggs and melted butter. Let ingredients cool if too hot and come to room temperature if too cold. Some of my early failures resulted from eggs added directly from the refrigerator.

Insert your thermometer in your loaves near the end of the process (this will not hurt the rise). Look for 190°F (88°C) for regular loaves, 200°F (93°C) for enriched (sweet) loaves, 205°F (96°C) for gluten-free bread, and 210°F (99°C) for denser bread, such as rye loaves. If you live in a high-altitude area, drop all the desired temperatures by 5°F (2°C) to adjust for the lower boiling point of water.

Step-by-Step Bread Machine Baking

If your bread machine, and breadmaking in general, is an old friend, you might skip this section. Creating bread is a science, and chemical and biological reactions are required for every aspect of the loaf from the rise to the crust. These reactions still need to occur even when using a bread machine; the difference is that they occur in the bucket rather than by hand. Read your manual for the basic breadmaking steps, keeping in mind there can be slight variations between brands.

Knowing what happens in the bread machine after you hit the Start button is not necessary to enjoy the golden, delicious loaves that pop out at the end of the program. But if you like to have heaps of information, here is the step-by-step process and a broad overview of the breadmaking (for Basic, Whole Wheat, Sweet, and French Cycles).

1. When the sourdough starter is ready (see page 17), you can make some bread!

2. Take the bread machine out of the packaging and read the manual. Wash the paddles and bucket in warm soapy water, dry them, and secure the paddles in the bucket. Wipe the inside of the lid with a damp cloth. Place the machine on a stable surface with lots of room around and above it.

3. Pick a recipe, read it through, and gather (purchase) the needed ingredients. Feed and activate the sourdough starter and bring the ingredients to room temperature.

4. Remove the bucket from the machine—ingredients can spill into the machine near the heating element while adding them to the bucket. Place the ingredients in the bucket in the order specified in the recipe or by the manufacturer. The recipes in this book use liquid, sweetener, salt, dry, and finally the yeast. Put the bucket back in the machine and close the lid.

5. Plug the bread machine into the outlet and choose the recipe program, including the loaf size and crust color. Your manual should have a detailed description of these settings. Press "Start" to begin the program.

6. The machine will follow its program; the first action will be mixing for about 4 minutes, then autolyze, which lasts 15 to 30 minutes, where the dough sits so the gluten can hydrate, and the gluten network can start to form. Open the lid and check the dough. You might need to add more water if it is too dry or more flour if too sticky.

7. The machine will knead the dough for 25 to 40 minutes until elastic and smooth by alternating paddle directions. If your machine has a signal to add fruit, nuts, and other ingredients, it will sound 10 minutes into kneading.

8. The temperature in the machine will rise a few degrees as it goes into bulk fermentation or first rise. This rise is about 1 hour and 10 minutes with a "punch down" (turn of the paddles) at about 40 minutes. Then the dough continues to rise with a second "punch down" at the end; you will hear the paddles turn.

9. Open the lid after the second "punch down," scoop the dough out, and remove the paddles. Shape the dough into a uniform, smooth loaf, and place it back in the machine. You can brush the top of the loaf at this point with a glaze, milk, or an egg wash and sprinkle on flaky salt or sesame seeds. Close the lid and let the program run its course.

10. The final rise lasts about 50 minutes, and then the machine increases the temperature to reflect the program, size of the loaf, and crust color. Baking takes between 50 minutes and 1 hour. Baking will seem effortless in the bread machine bucket, but it is a complex process. Your dough will expand one last time before the yeast is killed by the heat. The crust should form later in the bake so that the dough has an opportunity for that final expansion. As the bread bakes, the trapped carbon dioxide escapes from the dough, and the bread will retain its structure if the gluten network is strong and set.

11. When the machine signals the end of the cycle, turn the machine off and unplug it. Some machines will go into a "Warm" setting if you don't shut it off. I personally don't like it because the bread softens and I like a nice crust.

12. Remove the bucket (if removable) with oven mitts, turn it over, and slide the loaf out. Cool the bread on a raised wire rack. If the bread is stuck, tap the edge of the bucket on the counter, but do not run a knife around the loaf, or you might damage the bucket coating.

13. Cool the bread for as long as you can resist it. The longer, the better because the loaf will compress if you slice it while hot, and the texture will not be as lovely.

14. Store the cooled loaf in a sealed plastic bag at room temperature for up to 5 days, refrigerate for up to 1 week, or freeze for 3 months.

STORING DOUGH

The recipes in this book can be made using the dough program and stored to finish another day in the oven. To refrigerate, transfer the dough to a sealable freezer bag or a lightly oiled bowl. Seal or cover, and place in the fridge for up to 3 days. Punch the dough down once a day, or it can rise out of control—you only forget once! When ready to bake, take the dough out, shape it, let it rise, and bake. Or freeze the dough in a sealed plastic bag for up to 3 months. When you want to make a loaf, thaw the dough in the fridge overnight and follow the exact instructions as for chilled dough.

Caring for Your Bread Machine

I finally had to replace my bread machine recently after using my original one for more than nine years. The trick to a long relationship with your bread machine is cleaning and maintaining it after each use. You will find excellent information about caring for your device in the manual, but here is my routine:

- Do not place any machine components in the dishwasher. Wash them by hand with mild detergent and warm water, then dry thoroughly to prevent rust. Take out the paddles completely (if possible) and wash off clinging or baked-on dough.

- Do not clean the machine unless it is cool and unplugged.

- Do not use anything metal in the machine, such as spatulas or knives. Scratches in the bucket damage the nonstick surface.

- Do wipe or vacuum out any flour or crumbs in the bottom of the bread machine around the heating element.

- Do wipe the exterior with a damp cloth.

- Do oil the bread shaft spindle (on the outside of the bucket) with a couple drops of sewing machine oil every 6 months.

SAFETY TIPS

Although bread machines are relatively straightforward devices, always read the manual front to back before making your first loaf. Besides the safety instructions included in the manual, here are a few of my top tips to ensure your breadmaking experience is positive:

- Do place the machine on a stable, flat spot away from the walls—to keep vents clear—and the edge—some machines vibrate during kneading.

- Do tuck the cord safely away so it is away from hot elements and does not dangle over the edge of a counter where it can get snagged. Do not leave the bread machine plugged in when not in use.

- Do use oven mitts when handling the machine and its components (e.g., bucket, paddles, handle) after the baking program is complete.

Other Handy Tools

Besides your bread machine, some tools are required to create successful loaves or make the experience more enjoyable. Some are exclusively for finishing loaves in the oven, so don't run out and purchase those unless that is your plan. Nothing fancy is needed for the recipes in this book; you probably already have most items on this list in your kitchen.

FOR BREAD MACHINE AND OVEN LOAVES

Bowls: For proofing the dough and mixing washes. Glass bowls are best, but you can also use ceramic or wooden bowls in varying sizes.

Digital thermometer: A long-stemmed probe or instant-read thermometer is a very convenient tool when making bread (see Temperature in Breadmaking, page 36).

Knives: A serrated knife is essential for slicing bread cleanly, and a chef knife is used for chopping extra ingredients or making slashes in the loaves (if baking in the oven).

Measuring cups and spoons: You will need a set of dry and liquid cups and a set of measuring spoons.

Oven mitts: Heatproof oven mitts made of silicone or cloth are essential for handling the bucket from the bread machine, loaf pans, and loaves.

Pastry brush: Look for silicone brushes for egg washes to create a lovely crust or for brushing melted butter or glaze on finished loaves.

Scale: I do not measure the ingredients in this book by weight, although we have provided metric conversions, but you will undoubtedly come across recipes that strictly weigh ingredients.Purchase a scale that can weigh up to 5 pounds (2.3 kg) and switches from grams to ounces.

Wire cooling racks: Bread can get a soggy bottom if left to cool on the counter. A sturdy raised wire rack keeps air circulation around the loaf, so it cools evenly and stays crusty.

EXCLUSIVELY FOR OVEN LOAVES

Baking sheets: For all your needs, look for 10½- x 15-inch (26- x 38-cm) or 11- x 17-inch (28- x 43-cm), or 9½- x 12½-inch (25- x 32-cm) baking sheets made from heavy-gauge aluminum.

Kitchen towels: For covering the rising dough.

Mixing bowls: Have at a minimum 2 (4-quart or larger) bowls and 2 smaller bowls for proofing dough, making washes, and mixing fillings.

Plastic wrap: For covering the rising dough—either alone or with a large kitchen cloth.

Parchment paper or silicone mats: Prevents the bread from sticking to baking sheets or your Dutch oven.

Dutch oven: Look for a 5½-quart cast-iron (plain or enamel-coated) vessel with a tightly fitted lid.

Loaf pans: Look for 9- x 5-inch (23- x 13-cm) or 8½- x 4½-inch (22- x 12-cm) heavy-gauge nonstick aluminum loaf pans that have a dull surface.

MEASURING YOUR INGREDIENTS

Breadmaking falls under the baking umbrella, where precision is essential to success. You can certainly indulge in creative additions, but the foundation ingredients—flour, liquid, fat, sugar, salt, and yeast—must be accurate. So, expert measuring tools and techniques will come in handy.

First of all, make sure you have liquid and dry cups. You'll also need a set of spoons. If measuring by weight, you will need a scale. Weight is more accurate, but I have never had a serious issue using volume. Dry measuring cups have a flat top, and the measurement is to the very top so you can overfill it and then use a flat edge like a palette knife to level it off. Liquid measuring cups are see-through, so the line of the ingredient is visible. You might notice that the top line is not right at the top, so the liquid will not spill out.

To measure dry ingredients: Have you ever used a measuring cup to scoop flour right out of the bag? It might be a surprise to realize this is incorrect because you end up with too much—sometimes as much as 25 percent—because the flour is packed too tightly. The best method of measuring flour is to fluff the flour in the bag by stirring it and then spoon flour into the cup, so it is heaped over the top edge. Sweep a flat edge across the top to level the flour off. Measure other dry ingredients such as sugar (except brown sugar, usually packed), cocoa, coconut, and skim milk powder in the same way.

To measure liquids: Place the measuring cup on a flat surface and fill it to the desired measurement. Look at the cup at eye level, and you might notice the surface of the liquid is curved, higher at the sides than the middle. This is called a meniscus, and you measure from the bottom of the curve to be accurate.

Five Tips for Bread Machine Success

Besides the solutions in the troubleshooting section (page 45), here are my best tips for bread machine success:

- **Converting recipes to gluten-free and vice versa:** The gluten-free loaves created in a bread machine are more like quick bread and the dough more like a batter. The machine mixes the ingredients until well hydrated, and you will not see the same rising and kneading in the program. Swapping in gluten-free flour for regular and baking it on a gluten-free setting will produce a very unsatisfactory loaf and vice versa.

- **Check the dough:** Look at the dough as it is mixed and kneaded. If it is not a smooth ball, correct it by moving around the bucket so the dough does not stick to the sides. If too sticky, add flour by the teaspoon; if too dry, add water by the teaspoon. Also, never hesitate to remove the dough and feel it to assess its elasticity. Just avoid getting in the way of the paddles; they can pinch!

- **Use bread flour:** Canadian all-purpose flour contains as much protein as bread flour everywhere else, so I have never considered this issue. Look for bread flour and make sure it is at room temperature for the best results. I learned that the hard way after storing my flour in the freezer to keep it fresh.

- **Consider the ambient temperature:** This factor did not occur until several years into using my bread machine. I thought I was cleverly making bread in the machine during the hot, humid summer, with no added heat from the oven. However, my dough rose so high and fast, it knocked the lid up. If your kitchen is too hot, this will happen; the dough might not rise well if too cold. Consider baking another day if the weather is extreme.

- **Take the paddles out:** You don't have to do this, but the finished loaf is certainly easier to cut through the middle without a large, ragged hole. Take the paddles out before the final rise (your manual should tell you when), shape the dough into a neat loaf, and pop it back in the bucket.

HIGH-ALTITUDE BAKING

If you live in an area with an elevation of 3,000 feet (1 km) or higher, you will have to make a few adjustments. The air is thinner and drier, and the air pressure is lower, so moisture evaporates quickly, and your dough will rise faster.

The changes and experimentation required for a perfect loaf of bread might already be familiar if you bake regularly. If not, try all or a few of the following tweaks:

- Use a higher protein flour and increase the recipe amount by 1 tablespoon (weigh varies).

- Use colder ingredients to slow yeast action (so the dough doesn't rise as much).

- Use a smaller loaf setting on the bread machine to avoid over proofing.

- Reduce the yeast by ~ ½ teaspoon.

- Reduce the sourdough starter by 2 tablespoons to ¼ cup (about 40 to 60 g).

- Increase the liquid by 2 tablespoons (30 ml) per cup of flour (weight varies).

- Decrease the sugar, honey, or maple syrup by ~ ½ teaspoon.

- Increase the salt by ~ ¼ teaspoon.

- If finishing the loaf in the oven, increase the oven temperature by 25°F (15°C).

Troubleshooting

I remember one of the most experienced chefs I worked with telling me that baking bread was magic, and even if I followed the recipe precisely, the loaf might not be perfect. So many factors affect the various breadmaking steps, especially when throwing in sourdough starter and the bread machine. Don't stress; most "failed" loaves are still delicious. I employ a trial-and-error technique to determine the issue, changing one possible issue at a time until I achieve the results I want.

This section does not address possible bread machine trouble; check your manual or the brand website for mechanical fixes. Make sure you always have a licensed professional repair your bread machine for a safe resolution.

If your dough or bread does not look or feel quite right, here are some factors to consider:

DOUGH IS STICKY

Flour has a low gluten content
Kneaded too much
Not enough flour
Too much liquid

DOUGH IS DRY OR NOT COMING TOGETHER

Not enough liquid
Not kneaded enough
Too much flour

BREAD DOES NOT RISE ENOUGH

Cold ingredients
Incorrectly measured ingredients
The kitchen is too cold
Low gluten content in flour
Sourdough starter isn't strong enough or not fed and activated
Too little or too much sugar
Too much salt
Yeast came in contact with salt
Yeast is expired or inactive
Yeast killed by hot liquid

BREAD RISES TOO MUCH

Liquid temperature incorrect

Recipe size too big for the bucket size

Sourdough starter is very strong

Too little salt

Too much sourdough starter used

Too much yeast

BREAD TOO DENSE

Loaf is under-baked

Low gluten content in flour

Rise time or proofing too short

Too little liquid

Too little sourdough starter used

Too little sugar

Too little yeast

Too much whole grains, dried fruit, nuts, or seeds

Yeast is inactive

CRUST TOO THICK

Bread left in the machine too long

Low gluten content in flour

Too much sugar

Wrong program used

BREAD HAS A MUSHROOM TOP

Bread is overproofed

Bucket size is too small for the recipe

Too much liquid

Too much sourdough starter

Too much sugar

Too much yeast

COARSE TEXTURE OR LARGE HOLES

Fruit or vegetables too wet or in too large chunks

Too little salt

Too much flour

Too much liquid

Too much yeast

BREAD COLLAPSES

Bread machine opened after rise happens

Not enough salt

Too little yeast

Too much liquid

Too much sourdough starter

Wrong type of yeast

SOGGY BREAD

Bread left in the machine after baking

Humid weather

BREAD IS STRANGELY SHAPED

Bread is overproofed

Dough not kneaded enough

Oven temperature is too low

Too much flour

Too much yeast

PART TWO

The Recipes

The second part of this book contains seventy-three bread machine recipes, eleven shaped breads—dough created in the machine, bread or rolls finished in the oven—and twelve delicious discard recipes, so you don't waste a drop of your sourdough starter. The bread machine loaves are 2 pounds (908 g), made in my vertical bucket Black & Decker bread machine. I tested and tweaked every single one to achieve what I felt was the perfect result. Even with all that time spent making the recipes again and again, the bread was never precisely the same twice. Sometimes the starter was better activated, the kitchen too hot or too cold, the liquids slightly different temperatures, or perhaps the planets not aligned.

Many factors can change loaves, but I tell you, we ate every single one with enthusiasm. If the bread isn't perfect, try again another day or check out the troubleshooting section on page 45. As a final note, before you dive into the recipes, I believe cooking when happy and with passion is reflected in the bread; so, above all, have fun.

HOW TO CONVERT 2-POUND BREAD MACHINE RECIPES TO DIFFERENT SIZES

The recipes in this book all use a 2-pound setting. You can do a bit of math to convert each ingredient for other size loaves. If your calculation yields a strange measurement, round down or up to the nearest amount, such as ⅞ to 1 cup.

- Convert from 2 pounds (908 g) to 1 pound (454 g): Multiple by ½
- Convert from 2 pounds (908 g) to 1½ pounds (681 g): Multiply by ¾
- Convert from 2 pounds (908 g) to 2½ pounds (1.1 kg): Multiply by 1¼
- Convert from 2 pounds (908 g) to 3 pounds (1.36 kg): Multiply by 1½

CHAPTER THREE

Basic Loaves

These are my go-to loaves that I make at least once a week; they are straightforward, and for the most part, they don't include any fancy additions like cheese or chocolate. Despite the simplicity of the ingredients, you will find that these loaves are packed with heaps of flavor and boast lovely crusts. White, whole wheat, cracked wheat, and rye—light to dark—are all represented in this chapter. These recipes are a good place to start your sourdough bread journey.

TRADITIONAL SOURDOUGH BREAD

This is the first sourdough recipe I attempted in a bread machine, and much to my surprise, it turned out perfectly. Soft, golden crust with a lovely tang from the sourdough starter and a soft crumb. I sometimes add raisins and a half teaspoon of cinnamon to the recipe to jazz it up.

Makes:: 1 (2-pound/908 g) loaf (8 slices)	Prep time: 10 minutes	Total time: 3 hours 25 minutes

1 cup (225 to 235 g) white sourdough starter, fed, active, and at room temperature

¾ cup (175 ml) water (100°F to 110°F, or 38°C to 43°C)

1½ teaspoons canola oil

1½ teaspoons honey

1½ teaspoons sea salt

3 cups (360 g) white bread flour

1 teaspoon bread machine or quick active dry yeast

1. Place the starter, water, oil, honey, and sea salt in the bread machine's bucket, stirring slightly to combine. Add the flour and yeast. Program the machine for White/Medium Crust and press Start.

2. When the kneading cycles are complete, remove the paddles, reform the dough, and place it back in the bucket. Let the program continue until it is complete.

3. Cool the bread for 10 minutes, then remove it from the bucket and cool.

4. Store the bread in a sealed plastic bag at room temperature for up to 2 days, or freeze it in a sealed freezer bag for up to 2 months.

SOURDOUGH MILK BREAD

I lived in Amish country for a couple decades and enjoyed many delightful meals that featured signature milk bread. These traditional recipes create a slightly sweet, velvety crumb loaf perfect for toasting and dipping in soups and stews.

Makes: 1 (2-pound /908 g) loaf (8 slices)	Prep time: 10 minutes	Total time: 3 hours 25 minutes

1 cup (225 to 235 g) white sourdough starter, fed, active, and at room temperature

1 cup (240 ml) milk (100°F to 110°F, or 38°C to 43°C)

3 tablespoons (45 ml) melted butter, cooled

1 tablespoon (13 g) granulated sugar

1¼ teaspoons sea salt

4 cups (480 g) white bread flour

1½ teaspoons bread machine or quick active dry yeast

1. Place the starter, milk, butter, sugar, and sea salt in the bread machine's bucket, stirring slightly to combine. Add the flour and yeast. Program the machine for White/Medium Crust and press Start.

2. When the kneading cycles are complete, remove the paddles, reform the dough, and place it back in the bucket. Let the program continue until it is complete.

3. Cool the bread for 10 minutes, then remove it from the bucket and cool.

4. Store the bread in a sealed plastic bag at room temperature for up to 2 days, or freeze it in a sealed freezer bag with the air pressed out for up to 2 months.

WHOLE WHEAT SOURDOUGH BREAD

Whole wheat bread gets a bad reputation for being tasteless and having a rough mouthfeel. It is not as soft as white bread, but this recipe has a lovely, tender texture. Honey and butter enhance the nutty flavor of the whole wheat flour, but brown sugar or maple syrup are acceptable choices, as well.

Makes: 1 (2-pound/908 g) loaf (8 slices)	Prep time: 10 minutes	Total time: 3 hours 25 minutes

1½ cups (355 ml) water (100°F to 110°F, or 38°C to 43°C)

1 cup (225 to 235 g) whole wheat sourdough starter, fed, active, and at room temperature

2 tablespoons (30 ml) melted butter, cooled

1 tablespoon (20 g) honey

2 teaspoons (8 g) sea salt

4 cups (500 g) whole wheat flour

2 teaspoons (8 g) bread machine or quick active dry yeast

1. Place the water, starter, butter, honey, and sea salt in the bread machine's bucket, stirring slightly to combine. Add the flour and yeast. Program the machine for Whole Wheat/Medium Crust and press Start.

2. When the kneading cycles are complete, remove the paddles, reform the dough, and place it back in the bucket. Let the program continue until it is complete.

3. Cool the bread for 10 minutes, then remove it from the bucket and cool.

4. Store the bread in a sealed plastic bag at room temperature for up to 2 days, or freeze it in a sealed freezer bag with the air pressed out for up to 2 months.

LIGHT RYE SOURDOUGH

Any kind of rye bread is my first choice for sandwiches and breakfast; it might be my Dutch roots. The firm texture of this loaf is ideal for hefty sandwiches like Reubens or stacked corned beef creations. When you add sourdough to rye, the flavor becomes even more pleasingly complex.

Makes: 1 (2-pound/908 g) loaf (8 slices)	Prep time: 10 minutes	Total time: 3 hours 25 minutes

1¼ cups (281 to 294 g) white sourdough starter, fed, active, and at room temperature

1¼ cups (295 ml) warm water (100°F to 110°F, or 38°C to 43°C)

1½ teaspoons sea salt

2¼ cups (288 g) rye flour

2 cups (250 g) white bread flour

1 teaspoon instant dry yeast or bread machine yeast

1. Place the starter, water, and sea salt in the bread machine's bucket, stirring slightly to combine. Add the rye flour, white bread flour, and yeast. Program the machine for Whole Wheat/Medium Crust and press Start.

2. When the kneading cycles are complete, remove the paddles, reform the dough, and place it back in the bucket. Let the program continue until it is complete.

3. Cool the bread for 10 minutes, then remove it from the bucket and cool.

4. Store the bread in a sealed plastic bag at room temperature for up to 2 days, or freeze it in a sealed freezer bag with the air pressed out for up to 2 months.

SOFT SOURDOUGH SANDWICH BREAD

Everyone needs a perfect loaf for those quick, filling sandwiches that often get us through the day. This recipe produces a mild-flavored, soft-crumbed bread that is firm enough to cut into thin slices after it has cooled. You can add different ingredients to suit your palate, such as a sprinkle of fresh-cut herbs or even a handful of raisins, without compromising the structure of the bread.

Makes: 1 (2-pound/908 g) loaf (8 slices)	Prep time: 10 minutes	Total time: 3 hours 25 minutes

1¼ cups (281 to 294 g) white sourdough starter, fed, active, and at room temperature

¾ cup (175 ml) water (100°F to 110°F, or 38°C to 43°C)

1 tablespoon (13 g) granulated sugar

1 teaspoon sea salt

3¼ cups (390 g) white bread flour

1½ teaspoons instant dry yeast or bread machine yeast

1. Place the starter, water, sugar, and sea salt in the bread machine's bucket, stirring slightly to combine. Add the flour and yeast. Program the machine for White/Medium Crust and press Start.

2. When the kneading cycles are complete, remove the paddles, reform the dough, and place it back in the bucket. Let the program continue until it is complete.

3. Cool the bread for 10 minutes, then remove it from the bucket and cool.

4. Store the bread in a sealed plastic bag at room temperature for up to 2 days, or freeze it in a sealed freezer bag with the air pressed out for up to 2 months.

CRUSTY SOURDOUGH BREAD

This recipe is my one of my husband's favorites; it reminds him of the bread he enjoyed in Italy while playing hockey there in the 1980s. The shape is obviously square from the bread machine, but the finished loaf has a gorgeous defined crust more expected from the oven. Make sure it is completely cooled before storing it, or the steam will soften the crust.

Makes: 1 (2-pound/908 g) loaf (8 slices)	Prep time: 10 minutes	Total time: 3 hours 25 minutes

1 cup (240 ml) water (100°F to 110°F, or 38°C to 43°C)

1 cup (225 to 235 g) white sourdough starter, fed, active, and at room temperature

2 tablespoons (26 g) granulated sugar

1½ teaspoons sea salt

4 cups (480 g) white bread flour

1 teaspoon bread machine or quick active dry yeast

1. Place the water, starter, sugar, and sea salt in the bread machine's bucket, stirring slightly to combine. Add the flour and yeast. Program the machine for White/Medium Crust and press Start.

2. When the kneading cycles are complete, remove the paddles, reform the dough, and place it back in the bucket. Let the program continue until it is complete.

3. Cool the bread for 10 minutes, then remove it from the bucket and cool.

4. Store the bread in a sealed plastic bag at room temperature for up to 2 days, or freeze it in a sealed freezer bag with the air pressed out for up to 2 months.

HONEY SOURDOUGH BREAD

Honey is a lovely ingredient, and each choice creates a subtly different flavor in the bread. Try buckwheat, alfalfa, or lavender honey to find the one you like best. You can use butter instead of oil, but it will slightly mask the taste of the honey in the loaf.

Makes: 1 (2-pound/908 g) loaf (8 slices)	Prep time: 10 minutes	Total time: 3 hours 25 minutes

1 cup (225 to 235 g) white sourdough starter, fed, active, and at room temperature

¾ cup (175 ml) milk (100°F to 110°F, or 38°C to 43°C)

1 large egg, at room temperature, beaten

3 tablespoons (45 ml) canola oil

2 tablespoons (40 g) honey

1½ teaspoons sea salt

3¼ cups (390 g) white bread flour

1½ teaspoons bread machine or quick active dry yeast

1. Place the starter, milk, egg, oil, honey, and sea salt in the bread machine's bucket, stirring slightly to combine. Add the flour and yeast. Program the machine for White/Medium Crust and press Start.

2. When the kneading cycles are complete, remove the paddles, reform the dough, and place it back in the bucket. Let the program continue until it is complete.

3. Cool the bread for 10 minutes, then remove it from the bucket and cool.

4. Store the bread in a sealed plastic bag at room temperature for up to 2 days, or freeze it in a sealed freezer bag with the air pressed out for up to 2 months.

DANISH SOURDOUGH BREAD

Rugbrød is a traditional Danish loaf usually in a rectangle shape, so the bread machine doesn't alter its appearance too much. I add caraway seeds because I like the flavor; you can also add pumpkin seeds, sunflower seeds, and cracked rye kernels. There is no oil in this bread, so it is fewer calories and is slightly denser.

Makes: 1 (2-pound/908 g) loaf (8 slices)	Prep time: 10 minutes	Total time: 3 hours 25 minutes

1 cup (225 to 235 g) sourdough starter (white or rye), fed, active, and at room temperature

1½ cups (355 ml) water (100°F to 110°F, or 38°C to 43°C)

1 tablespoon (15 g) packed brown sugar

2 teaspoons (8 g) sea salt

2¼ cups (280 g) white bread flour

1¼ cups (160 g) rye flour

2 tablespoons (14 g) caraway seeds

1 teaspoon bread machine or quick active dry yeast

1. Place the starter, water, brown sugar, and sea salt in the bread machine's bucket, stirring slightly to combine. Add the white bread flour, rye flour, caraway seeds, and yeast. Program the machine for Whole Wheat/Medium Crust and press Start.

2. When the kneading cycles are complete, remove the paddles, reform the dough, and place it back in the bucket. Let the program continue until it is complete.

3. Cool the bread for 10 minutes, then remove it from the bucket and cool.

4. Store the bread in a sealed plastic bag at room temperature for up to 2 days, or freeze it in a sealed freezer bag with the air pressed out for up to 2 months.

DARK RYE SOURDOUGH

Dark rye flour is milled from the entire rye kernel—endosperm, sperm, and bran—creating a darker color and denser loaf. This flour also contains lots of fiber and fewer calories than wheat flour. This recipe contains about one-third white flour, but you can try 100 percent rye if you increase the yeast to 1¾ teaspoons.

Makes: 1 (2-pound/908 g) loaf (8 slices)	Prep time: 10 minutes	Total time: 3 hours 25 minutes

1 cup (240 ml) water (100°F to 110°F, or 38°C to 43°C)

¾ cup (168 to 177 g) sourdough starter (white or rye), fed, active, and at room temperature

1 tablespoon (15 g) packed brown sugar

1 teaspoon sea salt

2½ cups (320 g) dark rye flour

1½ cups (180 g) white bread flour

1¼ teaspoons bread machine or quick active dry yeast

1. Place the water, starter, brown sugar, and sea salt in the bread machine's bucket, stirring slightly to combine. Add the dark rye flour, white bread flour, and yeast. Program the machine for Whole Wheat/Medium Crust and press Start.

2. When the kneading cycles are complete, remove the paddles, reform the dough, and place it back in the bucket. Let the program continue until it is complete.

3. Cool the bread for 10 minutes, then remove it from the bucket and cool.

4. Store the bread in a sealed plastic bag at room temperature for up to 2 days, or freeze it in a sealed freezer bag with the air pressed out for up to 2 months.

ENGLISH MUFFIN SOURDOUGH BREAD

This loaf does not have English muffin nooks and crannies, but the flavor is very similar to this popular breakfast bread. The vinegar and baking powder create the taste, so don't exclude them! You will find the texture of this bread slightly spongy, and it should be cooled completely before slicing.

Makes: 1 (2-pound/908 g) loaf (8 slices)	Prep time: 10 minutes	Total time: 3 hours 25 minutes

1 cup (225 to 235 g) white sourdough starter, fed, active, and at room temperature

¾ cup (175 ml) milk (100°F to 110°F, or 38°C to 43°C)

½ cup (120 ml) water (100°F to 110°F, or 38°C to 43°C)

1½ tablespoons (25 ml) canola oil

1½ teaspoons granulated sugar

1¼ teaspoons sea salt

1 teaspoon white vinegar

½ teaspoon baking powder

3 cups (360 g) white bread flour

1¼ teaspoons bread machine or quick active dry yeast

1. Place the starter, milk, water, oil, sugar, sea salt, vinegar, and baking powder in the bread machine's bucket, stirring slightly to combine. Add the flour and yeast. Program the machine for White/Medium Crust and press Start.

2. When the kneading cycles are complete, remove the paddles, reform the dough, and place it back in the bucket. Let the program continue until it is complete.

3. Cool the bread for 10 minutes, then remove it from the bucket and cool.

4. Store the bread in a sealed plastic bag at room temperature for up to 2 days, or freeze it in a sealed freezer bag with the air pressed out for up to 2 months.

HONEY WHOLE WHEAT SANDWICH BREAD

A basic delicious sandwich loaf recipe is wonderful to have in your culinary repertoire. This bread has a rich flavor from butter, honey, and whole wheat flour. You can use it for PB&J, toasted tomato, and as a snack with a generous smear of butter.

Makes: 1 (2-pound/908 g) loaf (8 slices)	Prep time: 10 minutes	Total time: 3 hours 25 minutes

1 cup (225 to 235 g) white sourdough starter, fed, active, and at room temperature

¾ cup (175 ml) water (100°F to 110°F, or 38°C to 43°C)

2 tablespoons (30 ml) melted butter, cooled

2½ tablespoons (50 g) honey

1 teaspoon sea salt

2 cups (250 g) white bread flour

1½ cups (188 g) whole wheat flour

1 teaspoon bread machine or quick active dry yeast

1. Place the starter, water, butter, honey, and sea salt in the bread machine's bucket, stirring slightly to combine. Add the white bread flour, whole wheat flour, and yeast. Program the machine for Whole Wheat/Medium Crust and press Start.

2. When the kneading cycles are complete, remove the paddles, reform the dough, and place it back in the bucket. Let the program continue until it is complete.

3. Cool the bread for 10 minutes, then remove it from the bucket and cool.

4. Store the bread in a sealed plastic bag at room temperature for up to 2 days, or freeze it in a sealed freezer bag with the air pressed out for up to 2 months.

SOURDOUGH CRACKED WHEAT BREAD

Cracked wheat is coarsely ground wheat berries, and they add texture, nutty flavor, and heaps of fiber to bread. Using white bread flour as the base ingredient ensures you can see the cracked wheat when you slice the bread. Very pretty! If you pick up refined cracked wheat instead of regular, you can skip the soaking step.

Makes: 1 (2-pound/908 g) loaf (8 slices)	Prep time: 10 minutes	Total time: 3 hours 25 minutes

½ cup (70 g) cracked wheat kernels

1½ cups (355 ml) water (100°F to 110°F, or 38°C to 43°C)

1 cup (225 to 235 g) white sourdough starter, fed, active, and at room temperature

3 tablespoons (60 g) maple syrup

2 tablespoons (30 ml) canola oil

1½ teaspoons sea salt

3 cups (360 g) white bread flour

1 cup (125 g) whole wheat flour

1¼ teaspoons instant dry yeast or bread machine yeast

1. Place the cracked wheat in a small bowl and cover with boiling water by about 1½ inches (3.5 cm). Let stand until the kernels are tender, about 30 minutes.

2. Drain and add the kernels to the bread machine's bucket with the water, starter, maple syrup, canola oil, and sea salt. Stir to combine. Add the white bread flour, whole wheat flour, and yeast. Program the machine for Whole Wheat/Medium Crust and press Start.

3. When the kneading cycles are complete, remove the paddles, reform the dough, and place it back in the bucket. Let the program continue until it is complete.

4. Cool the bread for 10 minutes, then remove it from the bucket and cool.

5. Store the bread in a sealed plastic bag at room temperature for up to 2 days, or freeze it in a sealed freezer bag with the air pressed out for up to 2 months.

CHAPTER FOUR

Grain, Seed, and Nut Breads

When it comes to bread—for me, at least—the more texture, the better. I like the rough texture created by seeds, whole grains, and nuts because all those crevices and bumps hold the butter as it melts on a warm slice. Heaven! These loaves tend to be denser than basic bread, but they will still have a good rise, making them ideal for hearty sandwiches.

MULTIGRAIN SOURDOUGH BREAD

Multigrain cereal adds a bumpy, pleasing texture that catches butter as it melts on a warm slice of bread. I use Bob's Red Mill because the ratio seems ideal, but you can try your favorite brand or mix up your own. The extra yeast added to this recipe ensures it will rise even with the heavier grains in the dough.

Makes: 1 (2-pound/908 g) loaf (8 slices)	Prep time: 10 minutes	Total time: 3 hours 25 minutes

1 cup (225 to 235 g) white sourdough starter, fed, active, and at room temperature

¾ cup (175 ml) milk (100°F to 110°F, or 38°C to 43°C)

2½ tablespoons (38 ml) canola oil

3 tablespoons (45 g) packed brown sugar

1 teaspoon sea salt

2¼ cups (280 g) white bread flour

1¼ cups (200 g) multigrain cereal (Bob's Red Mill or equivalent)

1 cup (125 g) whole wheat flour

2 teaspoons (8 g) bread machine or quick active dry yeast

1. Place the starter, milk, oil, brown sugar, and sea salt in the bread machine's bucket, stirring slightly to combine. Add the white bread flour, multigrain cereal, whole wheat flour, and yeast. Program the machine for Whole Wheat/Medium Crust and press Start.

2. When the kneading cycles are complete, remove the paddles, reform the dough, and place it back in the bucket. Let the program continue until it is complete.

3. Cool the bread for 10 minutes, then remove it from the bucket and cool.

4. Store the bread in a sealed plastic bag at room temperature for up to 2 days, or freeze it in a sealed freezer bag with the air pressed out for up to 2 months.

OATMEAL SOURDOUGH BREAD

I have rolled oats, instant oats, and steel-cut oats in my pantry at all times; this ingredient shows up in many of my recipes, especially bread. Oats create a denser texture and slightly sweeter taste that is enhanced by the honey. Maple syrup would also be lovely in this loaf.

Makes: 1 (2-pound/908 g) loaf (8 slices)	Prep time: 10 minutes	Total time: 3 hours 25 minutes

1 cup (225 to 235 g) white sourdough starter, fed, active, and at room temperature

1 cup (240 ml) milk (100°F to 110°F, or 38°C to 43°C)

3 tablespoons (60 g) honey

2 tablespoons (30 ml) melted butter

1½ teaspoons sea salt

3 cups (360 g) white bread flour

1 cup (96 g) rolled oats

1¼ teaspoons instant dry yeast or bread machine yeast

1. Place the starter, milk, honey, butter, and sea salt in the bread machine's bucket, stirring slightly to combine. Add the flour, oats, and yeast. Program the machine for White/Medium Crust and press Start.

2. When the kneading cycles are complete, remove the paddles, reform the dough, and place it back in the bucket. Let the program continue until it is complete.

3. Cool the bread for 10 minutes, then remove it from the bucket and cool.

4. Store the bread in a sealed plastic bag at room temperature for up to 2 days, or freeze it in a sealed freezer bag with the air pressed out for up to 2 months.

SUNFLOWER SEED BROWN SOURDOUGH

Where I used to live, there was a field of sunflowers that stretched so far you could not see the far edges, and driving past it when in bloom was the highlight of my day. I think of that glorious sight when I use sunflower seeds in recipes like this one. These seeds add a wonderful nutty flavor and subtle texture to the loaf.

Makes: 1 (2-pound/908 g) loaf (8 slices)	Prep time: 10 minutes	Total time: 3 hours 25 minutes

1 cup (225 to 235 g) whole wheat sourdough starter, fed, active, and at room temperature

1 cup (240 ml) water (100°F to 110°F, or 38°C to 43°C)

3 tablespoons (45 ml) melted butter, cooled

1 tablespoon (13 g) granulated sugar

1¼ teaspoons sea salt

2½ cups (314 g) whole wheat flour

1½ cups (180 g) white bread flour

¾ cup (109 g) sunflower seeds

1¼ teaspoons instant dry yeast or bread machine yeast

1. Place the starter, water, butter, sugar, and sea salt in the bread machine's bucket, stirring slightly to combine. Add the whole wheat flour, white bread flour, sunflower seeds, and yeast. Program the machine for Whole Wheat/Medium Crust and press Start.

2. When the kneading cycles are complete, remove the paddles, reform the dough, and place it back in the bucket. Let the program continue until it is complete.

3. Cool the bread for 10 minutes, then remove it from the bucket and cool.

4. Store the bread in a sealed plastic bag at room temperature for up to 2 days, or freeze it in a sealed freezer bag with the air pressed out for up to 2 months.

NUTS AND SEEDS SOURDOUGH BREAD

The nuts and seeds in this recipe are my choices, but you can use pretty much any in the same quantities, such as pecans, pistachios, hazelnuts, or pumpkin seeds. Different choices create very different flavor profiles in the loaf. I like to use this bread for Gruyère or old Cheddar sandwiches.

Makes: 1 (2-pound/908 g) loaf (8 slices)	Prep time: 10 minutes	Total time: 3 hours 25 minutes

1 cup (225 to 235 g) white sourdough starter, fed, active, and at room temperature

1 cup (240 ml) water (100°F to 110°F, or 38°C to 43°C)

2 tablespoons (30 g) packed brown sugar

2 tablespoons (30 ml) canola oil

1 teaspoon sea salt

2½ cups (300 g) white bread flour

1 cup (125 g) whole wheat flour

1½ teaspoons instant dry yeast or bread machine yeast

¼ cup (28 g) chopped almonds

¼ cup (36 g) sunflower seeds

¼ cup (36 g) sesame seeds

1. Place the starter, water, brown sugar, oil, and sea salt in the bread machine's bucket, stirring slightly to combine. Add the white bread flour, whole wheat flour, and yeast. Program the machine for Whole Wheat/Medium Crust and press Start.

2. Add the almonds, sunflower seeds, and sesame seeds when the machine signals or the first kneading cycle is complete.

3. When the kneading cycles are complete, remove the paddles, reform the dough, and place it back in the bucket. Let the program continue until it is complete.

4. Cool the bread for 10 minutes, then remove it from the bucket and cool.

5. Store the bread in a sealed plastic bag at room temperature for up to 2 days, or freeze it in a sealed freezer bag with the air pressed out for up to 2 months.

MAPLE OAT SOURDOUGH

Maple and oats are a natural pairing, and the tanginess of the sourdough seems to highlight the sweetness of the syrup. You can also make this loaf 100 percent whole wheat or try 1 cup (128 g) of rye flour instead of 1 cup (120 g) of the white flour. This is the perfect choice for French toast if you have leftovers.

Makes: 1 (2-pound/908 g) loaf (8 slices)	Prep time: 10 minutes	Total time: 3 hours 25 minutes

1 cup (225 to 235 g) white sourdough starter, fed, active, and at room temperature

½ cup (120 ml) milk (100°F to 110°F, or 38°C to 43°C)

½ cup (120 ml) water (100°F to 110°F, or 38°C to 43°C)

¼ cup (60 ml) maple syrup

2 tablespoons (30 ml) melted butter, cooled

1½ teaspoons sea salt

3 cups (360 g) white bread flour

1½ cups (144 g) rolled oats

1½ teaspoons instant dry yeast or bread machine yeast

1. Place the starter, milk, water, maple syrup, butter, and sea salt in the bread machine's bucket. Add the flour, oats, and yeast. Program the machine for White/Medium Crust and press Start.

2. When the kneading cycles are complete, remove the paddles, reform the dough, and place it back in the bucket. Let the program continue until it is complete.

3. Cool the bread for 10 minutes, then remove it from the bucket and cool.

4. Store the bread in a sealed plastic bag at room temperature for up to 2 days, or freeze it in a sealed freezer bag with the air pressed out for up to 2 months.

SEEDED SOURDOUGH BREAD

I am the only one in my house that likes my bread with tons of seeds, so this loaf is all mine when it is popped out of the bread machine. Seeds create a subtle texture that cradles butter as it melts on a warm slice. They also add complex flavor and a decent boost of protein and healthy fats. Try hemp, chia, and poppy seeds in the mix for even more seedy goodness.

Makes: 1 (2-pound/908 g) loaf (8 slices)	Prep time: 20 minutes	Total time: 3 hours 25 minutes

1 cup (225 to 235 g) white sourdough starter, fed, active, and at room temperature

¾ cup (175 ml) milk (100°F to 110°F, or 38°C to 43°C)

1 tablespoon (20 g) honey

2½ teaspoons (10 g) active dry yeast

3 cups (360 g) white bread flour

2 tablespoons (18 g) sesame seeds

2 tablespoons (24 g) flaxseed

3 tablespoons (45 ml) melted butter, cooled

2 teaspoons (8 g) sea salt

1. Place the starter, milk, honey, and yeast in the bread machine's bucket, stir, and let stand 10 minutes.

2. Add the flour, sesame seeds, flaxseed, butter, and sea salt. Program the machine for White/Medium Crust and press Start.

3. When the kneading cycles are complete, remove the paddles, reform the dough, and place it back in the bucket. Let the program continue until it is complete.

4. Cool the bread for 10 minutes, then remove it from the bucket and cool.

5. Store the bread in a sealed plastic bag at room temperature for up to 2 days, or freeze it in a sealed freezer bag with the air pressed out for up to 2 months.

PECAN OAT SOURDOUGH

Pecans are the only nut tree indigenous to North America and essential to First Nations communities for many nutritious recipes. Freshly shelled pecans are best if you can find them or shell yourself. Pecans can stay fresh in the refrigerator for up to 8 months and in the freezer for up to 2 years.

Makes: 1 (2-pound/908 g) loaf (8 slices)	Prep time: 10 minutes	Total time: 3 hours 25 minutes

1 cup (240 ml) water (100°F to 110°F, or 38°C to 43°C)

¾ cup (168 to 177 g) white sourdough starter, fed, active, and at room temperature

¼ cup (32 g) skim milk powder

2 tablespoons (26 g) granulated sugar

2 tablespoons (30 ml) canola oil

1½ teaspoons sea salt

2 cups (250 g) white bread flour

1 cup (125 g) whole wheat flour

1 cup (96 g) rolled oats

1½ teaspoons instant dry yeast or bread machine yeast

½ cup (56 g) chopped pecans

1. Place the water, starter, skim milk powder, sugar, oil, and sea salt in the bread machine's bucket, stirring slightly to combine. Add the white bread flour, whole wheat flour, oats, and yeast. Program the machine for Whole Wheat/Medium Crust and press Start.

2. When the machine signals or the first kneading cycle is complete, add the pecans.

3. When the kneading cycles are complete, remove the paddles, reform the dough, and place it back in the bucket. Let the program continue until it is complete.

4. Cool the bread for 10 minutes, then remove it from the bucket and cool.

5. Store the bread in a sealed plastic bag at room temperature for up to 2 days, or freeze it in a sealed freezer bag with the air pressed out for up to 2 months.

FLAXSEED SOURDOUGH BREAD

You will find ground flaxseed and whole seeds here, so this is a hearty, nutritious bread. Flaxseed is rich in vitamins, minerals and is a stellar plant-based protein source. I prefer the golden seeds because the flavor is milder, but brown will work, as well.

Makes: 1 (2-pound/908 g) loaf (8 slices)	Prep time: 10 minutes	Total time: 3 hours 25 minutes

1½ cups (337 to 353 g) white sourdough starter, fed, active, and at room temperature

½ cup (120 ml) water (100°F to 110°F, or 38°C to 43°C)

2 tablespoons (30 ml) melted butter, cooled

2 tablespoons (40 g) maple syrup

1 teaspoon sea salt

2 cups (250 g) white bread flour

1½ cups (188 g) whole wheat flour

2 tablespoons (14 g) flaxseed meal

2 tablespoons (24 g) whole flaxseeds

1¼ teaspoons instant dry yeast or bread machine yeast

1. Place the starter, water, butter, maple syrup, and sea salt in the bread machine's bucket, stirring slightly to combine. Add the white bread flour, whole wheat flour, flaxseed meal, flaxseeds, and yeast. Program the machine for Whole Wheat/Medium Crust and press Start.

2. When the kneading cycles are complete, remove the paddles, reform the dough, and place it back in the bucket. Let the program continue until it is complete.

3. Cool the bread for 10 minutes, then remove it from the bucket and cool.

4. Store the bread in a sealed plastic bag at room temperature for up to 2 days, or freeze it in a sealed freezer bag with the air pressed out for up to 2 months.

BLACK WALNUT RYE SOURDOUGH

Most of the walnuts in grocery stores are English walnuts, which have a mild taste and thin shell. You can use English walnuts in this recipe if black walnuts are not available. Black walnuts have a bold, earthy flavor that creates a bread that almost tastes like dark rye.

Makes: 1 (2-pound/908 g) loaf (8 slices)	Prep time: 10 minutes	Total time: 3 hours 25 minutes

1 cup (225 to 235 g) rye sourdough starter, fed, active, and at room temperature

¾ cup (175 ml) water (100°F to 110°F, or 38°C to 43°C)

2 tablespoons (30 ml) canola oil

2 tablespoons (40 g) honey

1¼ teaspoons sea salt

1½ cups (180 g) white bread flour

1 cup (125 g) whole wheat flour

¾ cup (96 g) dark rye flour

1 teaspoon instant dry yeast or bread machine yeast

½ cup (60 g) chopped black walnuts

1. Place the starter, water, oil, honey, and sea salt in the bread machine's bucket, stirring slightly to combine. Add the white bread flour, whole wheat flour, dark rye flour, and yeast. Program the machine for Whole Wheat/Medium Crust and press Start.

2. When the machine signals or the first kneading cycle is complete, add the walnuts.

3. When the kneading cycles are complete, remove the paddles, reform the dough, and place it back in the bucket. Let the program continue until it is complete.

4. Cool the bread for 10 minutes, then remove it from the bucket and cool.

5. Store the bread in a sealed plastic bag at room temperature for up to 2 days, or freeze it in a sealed freezer bag with the air pressed out for up to 2 months.

SPELT SOURDOUGH BREAD

Spelt is an ancient grain that can be used in place of whole wheat flour in most recipes. It has a sweetish, nutty flavor, and is high in fiber, calcium, vitamin E, and B-complex vitamins. This recipe is lower in fat and calories than some other loaves because it doesn't contain fats or sweeteners.

Makes: 1 (2-pound/908 g) loaf (8 slices)	Prep time: 10 minutes	Total time: 3 hours 25 minutes

1 cup (225 to 235 g) white sourdough starter, fed, active, and at room temperature

¾ cup (175 ml) water (100°F to 110°F, or 38°C to 43°C)

1 teaspoon sea salt

2½ cups (247.5 g) wholemeal spelt flour

1½ cups (180 g) white bread flour

1 teaspoon instant dry yeast or bread machine yeast

1. Place the starter, water, and sea salt in the bread machine's bucket, stirring slightly to combine. Add the spelt flour, white bread flour, and yeast. Program the machine for Whole Wheat/Medium Crust and press Start.

2. When the kneading cycles are complete, remove the paddles, reform the dough, and place it back in the bucket. Let the program continue until it is complete.

3. Cool the bread for 10 minutes, then remove it from the bucket and cool.

4. Store the bread in a sealed plastic bag at room temperature for up to 2 days, or freeze it in a sealed freezer bag with the air pressed out for up to 2 months.

SESAME WHEAT BREAD

I use sesame products in lots of recipes because the smoky, rich taste delights me. That is why I double up on the flavor with both oil and seeds. A tablespoon (15 g) of tahini instead of the oil is also a nice touch. The scent of this bread baking is exotic, and you might not be able to wait until it cools before trying a piece.

Makes: 1 (2-pound/908 g) loaf (8 slices)	Prep time: 10 minutes	Total time: 3 hours 25 minutes

1 cup (225 to 235 g) whole wheat sourdough starter, fed, active, and at room temperature

1 cup (240 ml) water (100°F to 110°F, or 38°C to 43°C)

2 tablespoons (30 ml) canola oil

1 tablespoon (15 ml) sesame oil

1 tablespoon (20 g) honey

1 teaspoon sea salt

4 cups (500 g) whole wheat flour

¼ cup (36 g) sesame seeds

1½ teaspoons instant dry yeast or bread machine yeast

1. Place the starter, water, canola oil, sesame oil, honey, and sea salt in the bread machine's bucket, stirring slightly to combine. Add the flour, sesame seeds, and yeast. Program the machine for Whole Wheat/Medium Crust and press Start.

2. When the kneading cycles are complete, remove the paddles, reform the dough, and place it back in the bucket. Let the program continue until it is complete.

3. Cool the bread for 10 minutes, then remove it from the bucket and cool.

4. Store the bread in a sealed plastic bag at room temperature for up to 2 days, or freeze it in a sealed freezer bag with the air pressed out for up to 2 months.

PINE NUT BASIL SOURDOUGH

The basil pesto adds a pretty greenish hue to this bread and an excellent herbal taste. The pine nuts stay crunchy when baked, so each bite of the finished bread has a burst of texture. This loaf is my choice for toasted tomato sandwiches with a slice of mozzarella cheese; it tastes like a pizza!

Makes: 1 (2-pound/908 g) loaf (8 slices)	Prep time: 10 minutes	Total time: 3 hours 25 minutes

1 cup (225 to 235 g) white sourdough starter, fed, active, and at room temperature

¾ cup (175 ml) water (100°F to 110°F, or 38°C to 43°C)

2 tablespoons (30 ml) olive oil

1 tablespoon (20 g) honey

1 tablespoon (5 g) dried basil

1 teaspoon sea salt

3½ cups (420 g) white bread flour

1 teaspoon instant dry yeast or bread machine yeast

⅓ cup (45 g) pine nuts

1. Place the starter, water, oil, honey, basil, and sea salt in the bread machine's bucket, stirring slightly to combine. Add the flour and yeast. Program the machine for Whole Wheat/Medium Crust and press Start.

2. When the machine signals or the first kneading cycle is complete, add the pine nuts.

3. When the kneading cycles are complete, remove the paddles, reform the dough, and place it back in the bucket. Let the program continue until it is complete.

4. Cool the bread for 10 minutes, then remove it from the bucket and cool.

5. Store the bread in a sealed plastic bag at room temperature for up to 2 days, or freeze it in a sealed freezer bag with the air pressed out for up to 2 months.

CARAWAY RYE SOURDOUGH

Caraway seeds are a traditional ingredient in Scandinavian and Germanic cuisine, but these assertive seeds can be an acquired taste. These are actually the fruit of the caraway plant and not seeds at all. You can also use 2 teaspoons (4 g) of ground caraway if you don't enjoy the texture of whole seeds.

Makes: 1 (2-pound/908 g) loaf (8 slices)	Prep time: 10 minutes	Total time: 3 hours 25 minutes

1 cup (225 to 235 g) rye sourdough starter, fed, active, and at room temperature

1 cup (240 ml) water (100°F to 110°F, or 38°C to 43°C)

1½ teaspoons sea salt

2 cups (250 g) white bread flour

2 cups (256 g) light rye flour

1½ tablespoons (11 g) caraway seeds

1 teaspoon instant dry yeast or bread machine yeast

1. Place the starter, water, and sea salt in the bread machine's bucket, stirring slightly to combine. Add the white bread flour, rye flour, caraway seeds, and yeast. Program the machine for Whole Wheat/Medium Crust and press Start.

2. When the kneading cycles are complete, remove the paddles, reform the dough, and place it back in the bucket. Let the program continue until it is complete.

3. Cool the bread for 10 minutes, then remove it from the bucket and cool.

4. Store the bread in a sealed plastic bag at room temperature for up to 2 days, or freeze it in a sealed freezer bag with the air pressed out for up to 2 months.

FIG WALNUT SOURDOUGH BREAD

My first experience with figs was in North Africa, where I picked them ripe off the trees and ate them until my hands and face were sticky. This loaf uses dried figs instead of fresh, but the caramel flavor of the fruit shines through. If you can't find dried figs, dates will do in a pinch.

Makes: 1 (2-pound/908 g) loaf (8 slices)	Prep time: 10 minutes	Total time: 3 hours 25 minutes

1 cup (225 to 235 g) white sourdough starter, fed, active, and at room temperature

¾ cup (175 ml) water (100°F to 110°F, or 38°C to 43°C)

1¼ teaspoons sea salt

3 cups (360 g) white bread flour

1 teaspoon instant dry yeast or bread machine yeast

½ cup (75 g) chopped dried figs

½ cup (60 g) chopped English walnuts

1. Place the starter, water, and sea salt in the bread machine's bucket, stirring slightly to combine. Add the flour and yeast. Program the machine for White/Medium Crust and press Start.

2. When the machine signals or the first kneading cycle is complete, add the dried figs and walnuts.

3. When the kneading cycles are complete, remove the paddles, reform the dough, and place it back in the bucket. Let the program continue until it is complete.

4. Cool the bread for 10 minutes, then remove it from the bucket and cool.

5. Store the bread in a sealed plastic bag at room temperature for up to 2 days, or freeze it in a sealed freezer bag with the air pressed out for up to 2 months.

ALMOND SOURDOUGH BREAD

This loaf contains almonds in three ways—oils, extract, and sliced—and the resulting bread is fragrant and incredibly flavorful. I toast slices of this and top with cream cheese and marmalade.

Makes: 1 (2-pound/908 g) loaf (8 slices)	Prep time: 10 minutes	Total time: 3 hours 25 minutes

1 cup (225 to 235 g) white sourdough starter, fed, active, and at room temperature

¾ cup (175 ml) water (100°F to 110°F, or 38°C to 43°C)

2 tablespoons (40 g) honey

1 tablespoon (15 ml) almond oil

1 teaspoon sea salt

¼ teaspoon almond extract

2 cups (250 g) whole wheat flour

2 cups (250 g) white bread flour

1 teaspoon instant dry yeast or bread machine yeast

½ cup (56 g) sliced almonds

1. Place the starter, water, honey, almond oil, sea salt, and almond extract in the bread machine's bucket, stirring slightly to combine. Add the whole wheat flour, white bread flour, and yeast. Program the machine for Whole Wheat/Medium Crust and press Start.

2. When the machine signals or the first kneading cycle is complete, add the sliced almonds.

3. When the kneading cycles are complete, remove the paddles, reform the dough, and place it back in the bucket. Let the program continue until it is complete.

4. Cool the bread for 10 minutes, then remove it from the bucket and cool.

5. Store the bread in a sealed plastic bag at room temperature for up to 2 days, or freeze it in a sealed freezer bag with the air pressed out for up to 2 months.

WILD RICE SOURDOUGH

Wild rice is not rice at all; it is a semi-aquatic grass that grows in the Great Lakes region in North America. It has a nutty, earthy flavor and retains its firm texture when baked into bread. When you slice the loaf, tiny black flecks will be visible, creating a pleasing appearance.

Makes: 1 (2-pound/908 g) loaf (8 slices)	Prep time: 10 minutes	Total time: 3 hours 25 minutes

1 cup (225 to 235 g) white sourdough starter, fed, active, and at room temperature

¾ cup (175 ml) milk (100°F to 110°F, or 38°C to 43°C)

2 tablespoons (30 ml) melted butter, cooled

2 tablespoons (40 g) maple syrup

2 tablespoons (40 g) molasses

1 teaspoon sea salt

3½ cups (420 g) white bread flour

1 teaspoon instant dry yeast or bread machine yeast

1 cup (165 g) cooked wild rice

1. Place the starter, milk, butter, maple syrup, molasses, and sea salt in the bread machine's bucket, stirring slightly to combine. Add the flour and yeast. Program the machine for White/Medium Crust and press Start.

2. When the machine signals or the first kneading cycle is complete, add the wild rice.

3. When the kneading cycles are complete, remove the paddles, reform the dough, and place it back in the bucket. Let the program continue until it is complete.

4. Cool the bread for 10 minutes, then remove it from the bucket and cool.

5. Store the bread in a sealed plastic bag at room temperature for up to 2 days, or freeze it in a sealed freezer bag with the air pressed out for up to 2 months.

BARLEY SOURDOUGH BREAD

Barley comes in two types—hulled and pearled. Pearled is processed to remove the hull and bran, so it is softer and cooks quicker. Using this product means the grain basically bakes into the loaf, adding flavor and nutrition but less texture than the whole grain. This produces a denser, moist bread.

Makes: 1 (2-pound/908 g) loaf (8 slices)	Prep time: 10 minutes	Total time: 3 hours 25 minutes

1 cup (225 to 235 g) white sourdough starter, fed, active, and at room temperature

¾ cup (175 ml) water (100°F to 110°F, or 38°C to 43°C)

2 tablespoons (30 ml) canola oil

2 tablespoons (30 g) packed brown sugar

1 teaspoon sea salt

2½ cups (300 g) whole wheat flour

1 cup (120 g) white bread flour

1¼ teaspoons instant dry yeast or bread machine yeast

1 cup (157 g) cooked pearled barley

1. Place the starter, water, oil, brown sugar, and sea salt in the bread machine's bucket, stirring slightly to combine. Add the whole wheat flour, white bread flour, and yeast. Program the machine for Whole Wheat/Medium Crust and press Start.

2. When the machine signals or the first kneading cycle is complete, add the cooked barley.

3. When the kneading cycles are complete, remove the paddles, reform the dough, and place it back in the bucket. Let the program continue until it is complete.

4. Cool the bread for 10 minutes, then remove it from the bucket and cool.

5. Store the bread in a sealed plastic bag at room temperature for up to 2 days, or freeze it in a sealed freezer bag with the air pressed out for up to 2 months.

MUESLI SOURDOUGH BREAD

My mother made muesli for breakfast, and that dish inspired this crunchy, sweet loaf. You can use any type of granola, but the ones containing chocolate chips might not rise as much as a nut- and seed-based choice. If your granola is flavored with cinnamon, omit the spice in the recipe.

Makes: 1 (2-pound/908 g) loaf (8 slices)	Prep time: 10 minutes	Total time: 3 hours 25 minutes

1 cup (225 to 235 g) white sourdough starter, fed, active, and at room temperature

1 cup (240 ml) milk (100°F to 110°F, or 38°C to 43°C)

2 tablespoons (40 g) honey

2 tablespoons (30 ml) melted butter, cooled

1¼ teaspoons sea salt

½ teaspoon ground cinnamon

3 cups (360 g) white bread flour

1¼ teaspoons instant dry yeast or bread machine yeast

1 cup (110 g) store-bought granola

1. Place the starter, milk, honey, butter, sea salt, and cinnamon in the bread machine's bucket, stirring slightly to combine. Add the flour and yeast. Program the machine for White/Medium Crust and press Start.

2. When the machine signals or the first kneading cycle is complete, add the granola.

3. When the kneading cycles are complete, remove the paddles, reform the dough, and place it back in the bucket. Let the program continue until it is complete.

4. Cool the bread for 10 minutes, then remove it from the bucket and cool.

5. Store the bread in a sealed plastic bag at room temperature for up to 2 days, or freeze it in a sealed freezer bag with the air pressed out for up to 2 months.

CHAPTER FIVE

Fruit and Vegetable Breads

Adding fruits and vegetables to bread can be slightly tricky because these ingredients also add moisture, which can impede the rise. But don't be intimidated—the finished loaves are well worth the risk of a too-dense loaf, and the bread will still taste delicious! In this chapter, you will find recipes that use sweet potatoes and beets, finely chopped olives, tart lemons, plump berries, and even leftover mashed potatoes. The flavors will be exceptional, making these breads the ideal base for elaborate sandwich creations, though they are equally fabulous with just a thin smear of butter. Delicious!

GREEN OLIVE SOURDOUGH BREAD

My mother was European, so I've been eating olives my whole life; there was always a jar in the fridge. Their briny burst of flavor and firm texture add excitement to this crusty loaf of bread. If you enjoy olives on pizza or flatbread, this recipe might become a favorite.

Makes: 1 (2-pound/908 g) loaf (8 slices)	Prep time: 10 minutes	Total time: 3 hours 25 minutes

1 cup (240 ml) water (100°F to 110°F, or 38°C to 43°C)

¾ cup (168 to 177 g) white sourdough starter, fed, active, and at room temperature

1 tablespoon (15 ml) olive oil

1¼ teaspoons sea salt

3 cups (360 g) white bread flour

1¼ teaspoons instant dry yeast or bread machine yeast

½ cup (64 g) green olives, pitted and sliced

1. Place the water, starter, oil, and sea salt in the bread machine's bucket, stirring slightly to combine. Add the flour and yeast. Program the machine for White/Medium Crust and press Start.

2. When the machine signals or the first kneading cycle is complete, add the olives.

3. When the kneading cycles are complete, remove the paddles, reform the dough, and place it back in the bucket. Let the program continue until it is complete.

4. Cool the bread for 10 minutes, then remove it from the bucket and cool.

5. Store the bread in a sealed plastic bag at room temperature for up to 2 days, or freeze it in a sealed freezer bag with the air pressed out for up to 2 months.

SUNDRIED TOMATO BREAD

I have been known to eat an entire jar of sundried tomatoes as a snack by myself. I cannot overstate how much I love this ingredient, so obviously, I put it in bread whenever possible. When kneaded into the dough, some of the tomatoes will break down, so the loaf might have a slight pink color when baked.

Makes: 1 (2-pound/908 g) loaf (8 slices)	Prep time: 10 minutes	Total time: 3 hours 25 minutes

1 cup (240 ml) water (100°F to 110°F, or 38°C to 43°C)

1 cup (225 to 235 g) white sourdough starter, fed, active, and at room temperature

2 tablespoons (30 ml) olive oil

1 tablespoon (13 g) granulated sugar

1½ teaspoons sea salt

4 cups (480 g) white bread flour

1¼ teaspoons instant dry yeast or bread machine yeast

¾ cup (83 g) sliced oil-packed sundried tomatoes, pressed between paper towels to remove excess oil

1. Place the water, starter, oil, sugar, and sea salt in the bread machine's bucket, stirring slightly to combine. Add the flour and yeast. Program the machine for White/Medium Crust and press Start.

2. When the machine signals or the first kneading cycle is complete, add the sundried tomatoes.

3. When the kneading cycles are complete, remove the paddles, reform the dough, and place it back in the bucket. Let the program continue until it is complete.

4. Cool the bread for 10 minutes, then remove it from the bucket and cool.

5. Store the bread in a sealed plastic bag at room temperature for up to 2 days, or freeze it in a sealed freezer bag with the air pressed out for up to 2 months.

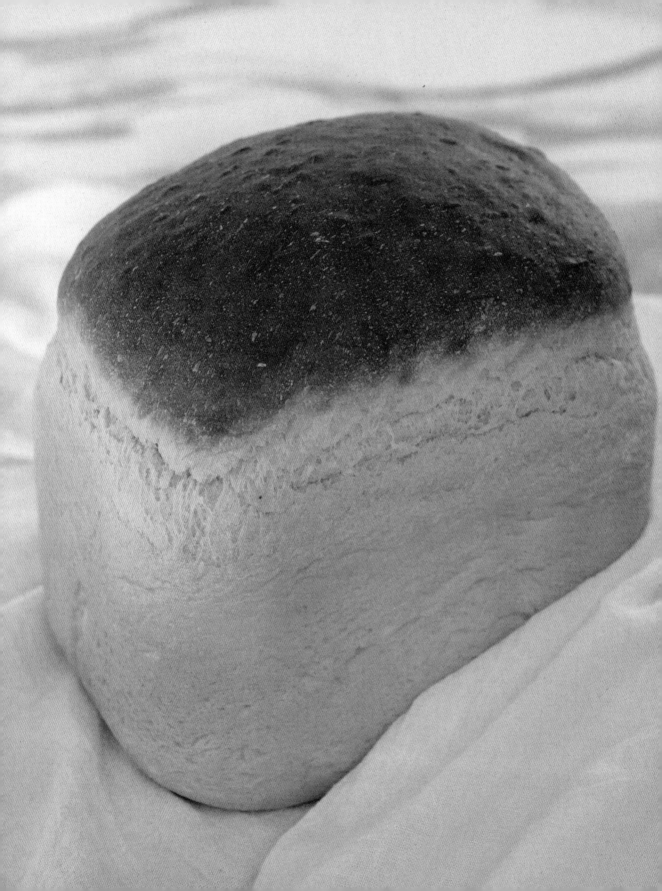

SWEET POTATO SOURDOUGH BREAD

Sweet potato creates a tender, distinctively hued bread with a lovely, sweet taste. Bring the mashed potato to room temperature before adding it to the bread machine, or the loaf will not rise enough. You can also try canned puréed pumpkin or mashed cooked butternut squash in this recipe.

Makes: 1 (2-pound/908 g) loaf (8 slices)	Prep time: 10 minutes	Total time: 3 hours 25 minutes

1 cup (225 to 235 g) white sourdough starter, fed, active, and at room temperature

1½ cups (338 g) mashed cooked sweet potato, at room temperature

½ cup (120 ml) milk (100°F to 110°F, or 38°C to 43°C)

2 tablespoons (40 g) honey

2 tablespoons (30 ml) melted butter, cooled

1 teaspoon sea salt

4 cups (480 g) white bread flour

1¼ teaspoons instant dry yeast or bread machine yeast

1. Place the starter, sweet potato, milk, honey, butter, and sea salt in the bread machine's bucket, stirring slightly to combine. Add the flour and yeast. Program the machine for Sweet/Medium Crust and press Start.

2. When the kneading cycles are complete, remove the paddles, reform the dough, and place it back in the bucket. Let the program continue until it is complete.

3. Cool the bread for 10 minutes, then remove it from the bucket and cool.

4. Store the bread in a sealed plastic bag at room temperature for up to 2 days, or freeze it in a sealed freezer bag with the air pressed out for up to 2 months.

SOURDOUGH BEET BREAD

I make a mess every time I prepare beets, especially as a chef. I ruined many chef coats with beet juice, but the flavor and color from these root veggies were worth the trouble. This bread is spectacularly gorgeous, perfect for dip platters or sandwiches. Its earthy flavor combines well with salmon salad or rare roast beef.

Makes: 1 (2-pound/908 g) loaf (8 slices)	Prep time: 10 minutes	Total time: 3 hours 25 minutes

1 cup (225 to 235 g) white sourdough starter, fed, active, and at room temperature

1 cup (244 g) beet purée

½ cup (120 ml) water (100°F to 110°F, or 38°C to 43°C)

2 tablespoons (30 ml) canola oil

1¼ teaspoons sea salt

4 cups (480 g) white bread flour

1¼ teaspoons instant dry yeast or bread machine yeast

1. Place the starter, beet purée, water, oil, and sea salt in the bread machine's bucket, stirring slightly to combine. Add the flour and yeast. Program the machine for White/Medium Crust and press Start.

2. When the kneading cycles are complete, remove the paddles, reform the dough, and place it back in the bucket. Let the program continue until it is complete.

3. Cool the bread for 10 minutes, then remove it from the bucket and cool.

4. Store the bread in a sealed plastic bag at room temperature for up to 2 days, or freeze it in a sealed freezer bag with the air pressed out for up to 2 months.

GARLIC AND BLACK OLIVE SOURDOUGH

Green olives were staples in my house, but I didn't try glossy black olives until I went to North Africa in my teens. They are not as briny, it seemed to me, and had an almost velvety texture. I love combining black olives with garlic to create this savory loaf.

Makes: 1 (2-pound/908 g) loaf (8 slices)	Prep time: 10 minutes	Total time: 3 hours 25 minutes

1 cup (225 to 235 g) white sourdough starter, fed, active, and at room temperature

1 cup (240 ml) water (100°F to 110°F, or 38°C to 43°C)

2 tablespoons (30 ml) olive oil

1 tablespoon (13 g) granulated sugar

2 teaspoons (6 g) minced garlic

1½ teaspoons sea salt

4 cups (480 g) white bread flour

1¼ teaspoons instant dry yeast or bread machine yeast

¾ cup (75 g) sliced black olives

1. Place the starter, water, oil, sugar, garlic, and sea salt in the bread machine's bucket, stirring slightly to combine. Add the flour and yeast. Program the machine for White/Medium Crust and press Start.

2. When the machine signals or the first kneading cycle is complete, add the olives.

3. When the kneading cycles are complete, remove the paddles, reform the dough, and place it back in the bucket. Let the program continue until it is complete.

4. Cool the bread for 10 minutes, then remove it from the bucket and cool.

5. Store the bread in a sealed plastic bag at room temperature for up to 2 days, or freeze it in a sealed freezer bag with the air pressed out for up to 2 months.

CORN SOURDOUGH

This is not the cakey cornbread you might be familiar with, but it does have that signature sweet taste. I use this bread as a container to serve spicy, thick chili by cutting out the top and center. I save that portion to use for dipping!

Makes: 1 (2-pound/908 g) loaf (8 slices)	Prep time: 10 minutes	Total time: 3 hours 25 minutes

1 cup (240 ml) water (100°F to 110°F, or 38°C to 43°C)

¾ cup (168 to 177 g) white sourdough starter, fed, active, and at room temperature

1 tablespoon (20 g) honey

1 teaspoon sea salt

3 cups (360 g) white bread flour

1 cup (126 g) corn flour

1¼ teaspoons instant dry yeast or bread machine yeast

1. Place the water, starter, honey, and sea salt in the bread machine's bucket, stirring slightly to combine. Add the white bread flour, corn flour, and yeast. Program the machine for White/Medium Crust and press Start.

2. When the kneading cycles are complete, remove the paddles, reform the dough, and place it back in the bucket. Let the program continue until it is complete.

3. Cool the bread for 10 minutes, then remove it from the bucket and cool.

4. Store the bread in a sealed plastic bag at room temperature for up to 2 days, or freeze it in a sealed freezer bag with the air pressed out for up to 2 months.

LEMON BLUEBERRY BREAD

Dried blueberries are found in almost every store and market where I live because these berries are plentiful in Canada. If you are not so lucky, try other dried berries such as cranberries or currants. This is fabulous bread for chicken salad sandwiches or toast with marmalade.

Makes: 1 (2-pound/908 g) loaf (8 slices)	Prep time: 10 minutes	Total time: 3 hours 25 minutes

1 cup (225 to 235 g) white sourdough starter, fed, active, and at room temperature

1 cup (240 ml) milk (100°F to 110°F, or 38°C to 43°C)

Juice and zest of 1 lemon

2 tablespoons (40 g) honey

2 tablespoons (30 ml) melted butter, cooled

1 teaspoon sea salt

4 cups (480 g) white bread flour

1½ teaspoons instant dry yeast or bread machine yeast

½ cup (73 g) dried blueberries

1. Place the starter, milk, lemon juice, lemon zest, honey, butter, and sea salt in the bread machine's bucket, stirring slightly to combine. Add the flour and yeast. Program the machine for Whole Wheat/Medium Crust and press Start.

2. When the machine signals or the first kneading cycle is complete, add the blueberries.

3. When the kneading cycles are complete, remove the paddles, reform the dough, and place it back in the bucket. Let the program continue until it is complete.

4. Cool the bread for 10 minutes, then remove it from the bucket and cool.

5. Store the bread in a sealed plastic bag at room temperature for up to 2 days, or freeze it in a sealed freezer bag with the air pressed out for up to 2 months.

WARM SPICED FRUIT SOURDOUGH

This seems like a fall or winter loaf; there is something festive about the taste. The scent of warm spices reminds me of the spice market in Tripoli, where vendors offered heaps of ingredients in a five-block radius. You can also use candied peel along with the dried fruit.

Makes: 1 (2-pound/908 g) loaf (8 slices)	Prep time: 10 minutes	Total time: 3 hours 25 minutes

1 cup (225 to 235 g) white sourdough starter, fed, active, and at room temperature

1 cup (240 ml) milk (100°F to 110°F, or 38°C to 43°C)

1½ tablespoons (25 ml) melted butter, cooled

1 tablespoon (20 g) molasses

1 teaspoon ground cinnamon

¼ teaspoon ground nutmeg

⅛ teaspoon ground cloves

1 teaspoon sea salt

3¾ cups (450 g) white bread flour

1¼ teaspoons instant dry yeast or bread machine yeast

1 cup (140 to 150 g) chopped or whole dried fruit (raisins, dried blueberries, dates, figs)

1. Place the starter, milk, butter, molasses, cinnamon, nutmeg, cloves, and sea salt in the bread machine's bucket, and stirring slightly to combine. Add the flour and yeast. Program the machine for Sweet/Medium Crust and press Start.

2. When the machine signals or the first kneading cycle is complete, add the dried fruit.

3. When the kneading cycles are complete, remove the paddles, reform the dough, and place it back in the bucket. Let the program continue until it is complete.

4. Cool the bread for 10 minutes, then remove it from the bucket and cool.

5. Store the bread in a sealed plastic bag at room temperature for up to 2 days, or freeze it in a sealed freezer bag with the air pressed out for up to 2 months.

CARAMELIZED ONION SOURDOUGH

This recipe has an extra step, but you can caramelize the onions up to three days ahead. Caramelized onions are sweet, smoky, and add golden flecks to the loaf. If you like onion buns, this recipe will delight you.

Makes: 1 (2-pound/908 g) loaf (8 slices)	Prep time: 20 minutes	Total time: 3 hours 25 minutes

For the Caramelized Onions

1 tablespoon (15 ml) olive oil

1 large Vidalia onion, peeled and chopped

¼ teaspoon sea salt

For the Bread

1 cup (225 to 235 g) white sourdough starter, fed, active, and at room temperature

1 cup (240 ml) water (100°F to 110°F, or 38°C to 43°C)

1 teaspoon sea salt

4 cups (480 g) white bread flour

1¼ teaspoons instant dry yeast or bread machine yeast

1. To make the caramelized onions, heat the oil in a medium skillet over medium heat. Sauté the onion until it is golden brown, about 8 minutes. Season with the salt and set aside to cool.

2. To make the bread, place the starter, water, and sea salt in the bread machine's bucket, stirring slightly to combine. Add the flour and yeast. Program the machine for White/Medium Crust and press Start.

3. When the machine signals or the first kneading cycle is complete, add the cooled onion.

4. When the kneading cycles are complete, remove the paddles, reform the dough, and place it back in the bucket. Let the program continue until it is complete.

5. Cool the bread for 10 minutes, then remove it from the bucket and cool.

6. Store the bread in a sealed plastic bag at room temperature for up to 2 days, or freeze it in a sealed freezer bag with the air pressed out for up to 2 months.

DATE AND MAPLE BREAD

The combination of maple and dates is a double blast of caramel, balanced by a wee bit more salt. Depending on how small you chop your dates, the fruit might not stay in chunks when kneaded. Dates are actually fresh fruit, so they do not have the hard texture of raisins.

Makes: 1 (2-pound/908 g) loaf (8 slices)	Prep time: 10 minutes	Total time: 3 hours 25 minutes

1 cup (225 to 235 g) white sourdough starter, fed, active, and at room temperature

1 cup (240 ml) milk (100°F to 110°F, or 38°C to 43°C)

3 tablespoons (60 g) maple syrup

1 tablespoon (15 ml) canola oil

1¼ teaspoons sea salt

3 cups (360 g) white bread flour

1½ cups (188 g) whole wheat flour

1½ teaspoons instant dry yeast or bread machine yeast

½ cup (89 g) chopped dates

1. Place the starter, milk, maple syrup, oil, and sea salt in the bread machine's bucket, stirring slightly to combine. Add the white bread flour, whole wheat flour, and yeast. Program the machine for Whole Wheat/Medium Crust and press Start.

2. When the machine signals or the first kneading cycle is complete, add the dates.

3. When the kneading cycles are complete, remove the paddles, reform the dough, and place it back in the bucket. Let the program continue until it is complete.

4. Cool the bread for 10 minutes, then remove it from the bucket and cool.

5. Store the bread in a sealed plastic bag at room temperature for up to 2 days, or freeze it in a sealed freezer bag with the air pressed out for up to 2 months.

APPLE PIE SOURDOUGH BREAD

I grew up with two types of apple pies: my mom's sweet crumble-style and the standard lard-based crust version my nana put on the table every time we visited. This bread reminds me of both, not too sweet, lightly spiced, and buttery. You can try pear in the bread instead of apple with similar results.

Makes: 1 (2-pound/908 g) loaf (8 slices)	Prep time: 10 minutes	Total time: 3 hours 25 minutes

1 cup (225 to 235 g) white sourdough starter, fed, active, and at room temperature

¾ cup (175 ml) water (100°F to 110°F, or 38°C to 43°C)

1 tablespoon (15 ml) melted butter, cooled

1 tablespoon (15 g) packed brown sugar

1 teaspoon sea salt

½ teaspoon ground cinnamon

¼ teaspoon ground nutmeg

3 cups (360 g) white bread flour

1 cup (96 g) rolled oats

1½ teaspoons instant dry yeast or bread machine yeast

1 medium apple, peeled, cored, and finely chopped

1. Place the starter, water, butter, brown sugar, sea salt, cinnamon, and nutmeg in the bread machine's bucket, stirring slightly to combine. Add the flour, oats, and yeast. Program the machine for Whole Wheat/Medium Crust and press Start.

2. When the machine signals or the first kneading cycle is complete, add the apple.

3. When the kneading cycles are complete, remove the paddles, reform the dough, and place it back in the bucket. Let the program continue until it is complete.

4. Cool the bread for 10 minutes, then remove it from the bucket and cool.

5. Store the bread in a sealed plastic bag at room temperature for up to 2 days, or freeze it in a sealed freezer bag with the air pressed out for up to 2 months.

GOLDEN CARROT SOURDOUGH

The flavor and color of this bread come from carrot juice rather than grated vegetables. This choice is so the bread stays fluffy and rises high. Fresh carrot juice can be found in most grocery stores in the produce or refrigerated food section. You can make your own if you have a juicer.

Makes: 1 (2-pound/908 g) loaf (8 slices)	Prep time: 10 minutes	Total time: 3 hours 25 minutes

1 cup (225 to 235 g) white sourdough starter, fed, active, and at room temperature

1 cup (240 ml) carrot juice (100°F to 110°F, or 38°C to 43°C)

1 tablespoon (15 ml) canola oil

1 tablespoon (20 g) honey

1 teaspoon sea salt

3 cups (360 g) white bread flour

1 cup (125 g) whole wheat flour

1¼ teaspoons instant dry yeast or bread machine yeast

1. Place the starter, carrot juice, oil, honey, and sea salt in the bread machine's bucket, stirring slightly to combine. Add the white bread flour, whole wheat flour, and yeast. Program the machine for Whole Wheat/Medium Crust and press Start.

2. When the kneading cycles are complete, remove the paddles, reform the dough, and place it back in the bucket. Let the program continue until it is complete.

3. Cool the bread for 10 minutes, then remove it from the bucket and cool.

4. Store the bread in a sealed plastic bag at room temperature for up to 2 days, or freeze it in a sealed freezer bag with the air pressed out for up to 2 months.

ORANGE POPPY SEED SOURDOUGH

When I was a child, one of my favorite treats was a poppy seed strudel my mother picked up from a European market in the neighborhood. I loved that crunchy, bittersweet flavor, so I tried to replicate the taste profile here. The butter, honey, and orange combine with the poppy seeds to produce a sweeter bread.

Makes: 1 (2-pound/908 g) loaf (8 slices)	Prep time: 10 minutes	Total time: 3 hours 25 minutes

1 cup (225 to 235 g) white sourdough starter, fed, active, and at room temperature

1 cup (240 ml) milk (100°F to 110°F, or 38°C to 43°C)

Juice and zest of 1 orange

3 tablespoons (27 g) poppy seeds

3 tablespoons (60 g) honey

2 tablespoons (30 ml) melted butter, cooled

1 teaspoon sea salt

3¾ cups (450 g) white bread flour

1½ teaspoons instant dry yeast or bread machine yeast

1. Place the starter, milk, orange juice, orange zest, poppy seeds, honey, butter, and sea salt in the bread machine's bucket, stirring slightly to combine. Add the flour and yeast. Program the machine for Sweet/Medium Crust and press Start.

2. When the kneading cycles are complete, remove the paddles, reform the dough, and place it back in the bucket. Let the program continue until it is complete.

3. Cool the bread for 10 minutes, then remove it from the bucket and cool.

4. Store the bread in a sealed plastic bag at room temperature for up to 2 days, or freeze it in a sealed freezer bag with the air pressed out for up to 2 months.

ROASTED GARLIC SOURDOUGH

Roasted garlic is available premade in a purée in many stores, but it is better fresh. In the past, I often whipped up a big batch to spread on fresh bread, so I finally decided to put it right in the bread. You won't be disappointed by the smooth, rich flavor.

Makes: 1 (2-pound/908 g) loaf (8 slices)	Prep time: 10 minutes	Total time: 3 hours 25 minutes

1 cup (225 to 235 g) white sourdough starter, fed, active, and at room temperature

1 cup (240 ml) water (100°F to 110°F, or 38°C to 43°C)

2 tablespoons (30 ml) olive oil

2 tablespoons (30 g) roasted garlic purée

1¼ teaspoons sea salt

3½ cups (420 g) white bread flour

1¼ teaspoons instant dry yeast or bread machine yeast

1. Place the starter, water, oil, garlic purée, and sea salt in the bread machine's bucket, stirring slightly to combine. Add the flour and yeast. Program the machine for French/Medium Crust and press Start.

2. When the kneading cycles are complete, remove the paddles, reform the dough, and place it back in the bucket. Let the program continue until it is complete.

3. Cool the bread for 10 minutes, then remove it from the bucket and cool.

4. Store the bread in a sealed plastic bag at room temperature for up to 2 days, or freeze it in a sealed freezer bag with the air pressed out for up to 2 months.

POTATO DILL SOURDOUGH

Potato bread has a fine texture and distinct flavor, especially with the addition of dill. As with other recipes using puréed or mashed ingredients, make sure the potatoes are not cold when adding them to the bread machine. This bread can be further enhanced with a couple slices of chopped cooked bacon added when your machine signals.

Makes: 1 (2-pound/908 g) loaf (8 slices)	Prep time: 10 minutes	Total time: 3 hours 25 minutes

1 cup (225 to 235 g) white sourdough starter, fed, active, and at room temperature

1 cup (240 ml) milk (100°F to 110°F, or 38°C to 43°C)

¾ cup (169 g) mashed potatoes, at room temperature

1 tablespoon (13 g) granulated sugar

1 tablespoon (15 ml) melted butter, cooled

1 tablespoon (3 g) dried dill

1½ teaspoons sea salt

3 cups (360 g) white bread flour

1 cup (128 g) light rye flour

1½ teaspoons instant dry yeast or bread machine yeast

1. Place the starter, milk, mashed potatoes, sugar, butter, dill, and sea salt in the bread machine's bucket, stirring slightly to combine. Add the white bread flour, rye flour, and yeast. Program the machine for Whole Wheat/Medium Crust and press Start.

2. When the kneading cycles are complete, remove the paddles, reform the dough, and place it back in the bucket. Let the program continue until it is complete.

3. Cool the bread for 10 minutes, then remove it from the bucket and cool.

4. Store the bread in a sealed plastic bag at room temperature for up to 2 days, or freeze it in a sealed freezer bag with the air pressed out for up to 2 months.

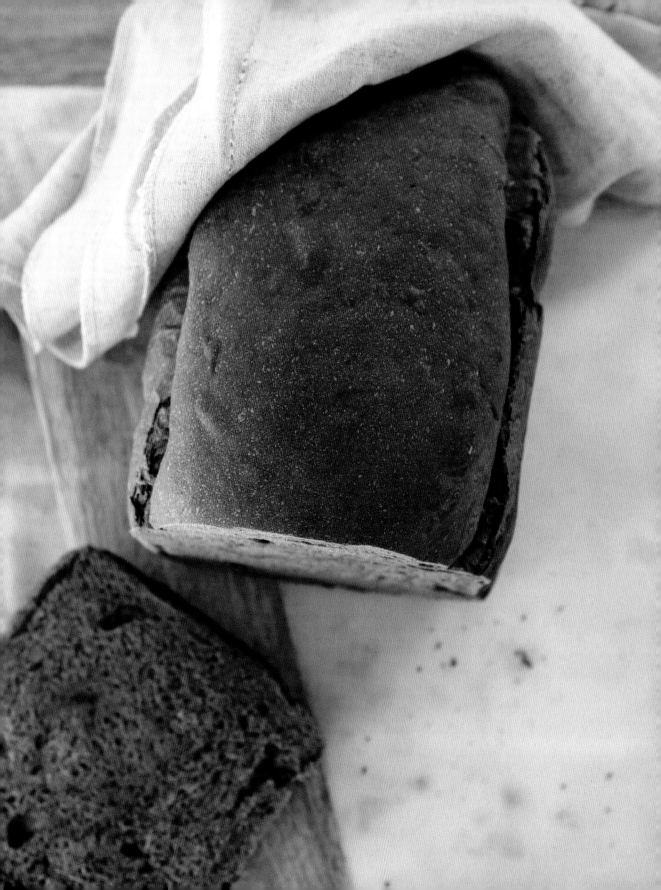

CHAPTER SIX

Sweet Breads

Some of my favorite loaves are sweet breads such as brioche, chocolate babka, and barmbrack, which is consumed within an hour of baking by myself and my sons. These recipes include many traditional favorites and beloved flavor combinations, but they can be tricky due to the additional quantities of butter and sugar. Using the Sweet program on your machine ensures the baking temperature and time reflect these ingredients, so jump right in and enjoy the delicious results.

PANETTONE

Panettone is a delight, a traditional Italian holiday bread enjoyed at Christmas and New Year's. It is sweet, tender, and studded with tart currants. The orange zest adds lovely colored flecks and a wonderful flavor. For a real treat, add 3 ½ cups (87 g) of chopped white chocolate along with the currants.

Makes: 1 (2-pound/908 g) loaf (8 slices)	Prep time: 10 minutes	Total time: 3 hours 25 minutes

1 cup (225 to 235 g) white sourdough starter, fed, active, and at room temperature

½ cup (120 ml) milk (100°F to 110°F, or 38°C to 43°C)

1 large egg, at room temperature, beaten

3 tablespoons (45 ml) melted butter, cooled

3 tablespoons (39 g) granulated sugar

1 tablespoon (6 g) orange zest

1½ teaspoons sea salt

3 cups (360 g) white bread flour

1¼ teaspoons instant dry yeast or bread machine yeast

½ cup (75 g) dried currants

½ cup (70 g) candied citrus peel

1. Place the starter, milk, egg, butter, sugar, orange zest, and sea salt in the bread machine's bucket, stirring slightly to combine. Add the flour and yeast. Program the bread machine for Sweet/Medium Crust and press Start.

2. When the machine signals or the first kneading cycle is done, add the currants and citrus peel.

3. When the kneading cycles are complete, remove the paddles, reform the dough, and place it back in the bucket. Let the program continue until it is complete.

4. When the loaf is done, remove the bucket from the bread machine. Let the loaf cool for 5 minutes, then turn the bucket upside down and gently shake it to remove the loaf and turn it out onto a rack to cool.

5. Store the bread in a sealed plastic bag at room temperature for up to 4 days, or freeze it in a sealed plastic bag with the air pressed out for up to 2 months.

BRIOCHE

One of my most cherished cooking memories is making brioche with a tiny French chef named Francis, who once cooked at the White House in the 1970s. We used his ten-year-old sourdough starter, and he explained the importance of adding the butter after the first knead. This bread machine recipe would make him proud.

Makes: 1 (2-pound/908 g) loaf (8 slices)	Prep time: 10 minutes	Total time: 3 hours 25 minutes

1 cup (225 to 235 g) white sourdough starter, fed, active, and at room temperature

½ cup (120 ml) milk (100°F to 110°F, or 38°C to 43°C)

3 large eggs, at room temperature, beaten

2 tablespoons (26 g) granulated sugar

1 teaspoon sea salt

3½ cups (420 g) white bread flour

1½ teaspoons instant dry yeast or bread machine yeast

¾ cup (168 g) butter, softened, in 1-inch (2.5-cm) chunks

1. Place the starter, milk, eggs, sugar, and sea salt in the bread machine's bucket, stirring slightly to combine. Add the flour and yeast. Program the machine for Sweet/Medium Crust and press Start.

2. When the machine signals or the first kneading cycle is complete, add the butter in chunks until incorporated.

3. When the kneading cycles are complete, remove the paddles, reform the dough, and place it back in the bucket. Let the program continue until it is complete.

4. Cool the bread for 10 minutes, then remove it from the bucket and cool.

5. Store the bread in a sealed plastic bag at room temperature for up to 2 days, or freeze it in a sealed freezer bag with the air pressed out for up to 2 months.

CHOCOLATE CINNAMON BREAD

One day, I was craving a sweet treat but did not have all the ingredients I needed for brownies, so this loaf was my compromise. I patiently waited while it baked, and the warm scent of cinnamon and chocolate filled my house. It was spectacular warm with a bit of butter and equally fabulous the next day when I used it for French toast.

Makes: 1 (2-pound/908 g) loaf (8 slices)	Prep time: 10 minutes	Total time: 3 hours 25 minutes

1 cup (225 to 235 g) white sourdough starter, fed, active, and at room temperature

¾ cup (175 ml) milk (100°F to 110°F, or 38°C to 43°C)

¼ cup (22 g) cocoa powder

3 tablespoons (39 g) granulated sugar

2 tablespoons (30 ml) melted butter, cooled

1½ teaspoons sea salt

1 teaspoon ground cinnamon

3½ cups (420 g) white bread flour

1½ teaspoons instant dry yeast or bread machine yeast

½ cup (87 g) semisweet chocolate chips

1. Place the starter, milk, cocoa powder, sugar, butter, sea salt, and cinnamon in the bread machine's bucket. Add the flour and yeast. Program the machine for Sweet/Medium Crust and press Start.

2. When the machine signals or the first kneading cycle is done, add the chocolate chips.

3. When the kneading cycles are complete, remove the paddles, reform the dough, and place it back in the bucket. Let the program continue until it is complete.

4. When the loaf is done, remove the bucket from the machine. Let the loaf cool for 5 minutes, then gently shake the pan to remove the loaf and turn it out onto a rack to cool.

5. Store the bread in a sealed plastic bag at room temperature for up to 5 days, or freeze it in a sealed plastic bag with the air pressed out for up to 2 months.

ORANGE VANILLA SOURDOUGH

Sweet bread is my dessert; I would rather eat this vanilla- and citrus-infused tender bread than a cheesecake or cookies. The milk, honey, and butter create a gorgeous rich flavor and a pretty, golden crust ideal for French toast or slathered with a bit of butter as a snack. For an even more robust vanilla flavor, try scraping a vanilla bean's seeds into the wet ingredients instead of using an extract.

Makes: 1 (2-pound/908 g) loaf (8 slices)	Prep time: 10 minutes	Total time: 3 hours 25 minutes

1¼ cups (281 to 294 g) white sourdough starter, fed, active, and at room temperature

½ cup (120 ml) milk (100°F to 110°F, or 38°C to 43°C)

Juice and zest of 1 orange

¼ cup (85 g) honey

1 large egg, at room temperature, beaten

¼ cup (60 ml) melted butter, cooled

2 teaspoons (8 g) sea salt

1 teaspoon vanilla extract

4 cups (480 g) white bread flour

2 teaspoons (8 g) instant dry yeast or bread machine yeast

1. Place the starter, milk, orange juice, orange zest, honey, egg, butter, sea salt, and vanilla in the bread machine's bucket. Add the flour and yeast. Program the machine for Sweet/Light Crust, and press Start.

2. When the kneading cycles are complete, remove the paddles, reform the dough, and place it back in the bucket. Let the program continue until it is complete.

3. Let the bread cool for 10 minutes, then remove the loaf and turn it out onto a rack to cool.

4. Store the bread in a sealed plastic bag in the refrigerator for up to 4 days, or freeze it in a sealed freezer bag with the air pressed out for up to 2 months.

BUTTERY CINNAMON SOURDOUGH

You will be reminded of cinnamon rolls when you bite into this fragrant, sweet bread. The addition of eggs ensures a tender pull-apart texture, and brown sugar adds a subtle caramel flavor. This bread is lovely if you substitute 1 cup (125 g) of whole wheat flour for 1 cup (120 g) of the white flour.

Makes: 1 (2-pound/908 g) loaf (8 slices)	Prep time: 10 minutes	Total time: 3 hours 25 minutes

1 cup (225 to 235 g) white sourdough starter, fed, active, and at room temperature

1 cup (240 ml) milk (100°F to 110°F, or 38°C to 43°C)

3 large eggs, at room temperature, beaten

¼ cup (60 ml) melted butter, cooled

3 tablespoons (45 g) packed brown sugar

1½ teaspoons ground cinnamon

1¼ teaspoons sea salt

4 cups (480 g) white bread flour

1½ teaspoons instant dry yeast or bread machine yeast

1. Place the starter, milk, eggs, butter, brown sugar, cinnamon, and sea salt in the bread machine's bucket. Add the flour and yeast. Program the machine for Sweet/Light Crust, and press Start.

2. When the kneading cycles are complete, remove the paddles, reform the dough, and place it back in the bucket. Let the program continue until it is complete.

3. Let the bread cool for 10 minutes, then remove the loaf and turn it out onto a rack to cool.

4. Store the bread in a sealed plastic bag in the refrigerator for up to 4 days, or freeze it in a sealed freezer bag with the air pressed out for up to 2 months.

SOURDOUGH MILK CHOCOLATE BABKA

I admit chocolate is a staple in my home, so I am constantly looking to add it to recipes. Why not bread? This babka does not have distinctive swirly chocolate layers, but the flavor is surprisingly authentic. You can swap in dark or semisweet chocolate for milk chocolate if that suits you better.

Makes: 1 (2-pound/908 g) loaf (8 slices)	Prep time: 10 minutes	Total time: 3 hours 25 minutes

1 cup (225 to 235 g) white sourdough starter, fed, active, and at room temperature

½ cup (120 ml) milk (100°F to 110°F, or 38°C to 43°C)

2 large eggs, at room temperature, beaten

¼ cup (50 g) granulated sugar

¼ cup (60 ml) melted butter, cooled

1 teaspoon sea salt

4 cups (480 g) white bread flour

1½ teaspoons instant dry yeast or bread machine yeast

1 cup (175 g) roughly chopped good-quality milk chocolate

1. Place the starter, milk, eggs, sugar, butter, and sea salt in the bread machine's bucket, stirring slightly to combine. Add the flour and yeast. Program the machine for Sweet/Medium Crust and press Start.

2. When the machine signals or the first kneading cycle is complete, add the chocolate.

3. When the kneading cycles are complete, remove the paddles, reform the dough, and place it back in the bucket. Let the program continue until it is complete.

4. Cool the bread for 10 minutes, then remove it from the bucket and cool.

5. Store the bread in a sealed plastic bag at room temperature for up to 2 days, or freeze it in a sealed freezer bag with the air pressed out for up to 2 months.

YOGURT HONEY SOURDOUGH

Adding Greek yogurt to this tasty loaf boosts the tangy sourdough flavor and creates a beautiful, tender texture. Vanilla- or coconut-flavored yogurt would also complement the honey and butter accents in the bread. I love this one in the morning with homemade strawberry jam.

Makes: 1 (2-pound/908 g) loaf (8 slices)	Prep time: 10 minutes	Total time: 3 hours 25 minutes

1 cup (225 to 235 g) white sourdough starter, fed, active, and at room temperature

1 cup (240 ml) milk (100°F to 110°F, or 38°C to 43°C)

½ cup (100 g) plain Greek yogurt

3 tablespoons (60 g) honey

2 tablespoons (30 ml) melted butter, cooled

1¼ teaspoons sea salt

3½ cups (420 g) white bread flour

1½ teaspoons instant dry yeast or bread machine yeast

1. Place the starter, milk, yogurt, honey, butter, and sea salt in the bread machine's bucket, stirring slightly to combine. Add the flour and yeast. Program the machine for Sweet/Medium Crust and press Start.

2. When the kneading cycles are complete, remove the paddles, reform the dough, and place it back in the bucket. Let the program continue until it is complete.

3. Cool the bread for 10 minutes, then remove it from the bucket and cool.

4. Store the bread in a sealed plastic bag at room temperature for up to 2 days, or freeze it in a sealed freezer bag with the air pressed out for up to 2 months.

MAPLE COFFEE BREAD

I live in Northern Ontario, Canada, where maple syrup is famous, and we often sneak a teaspoon or two just to get a treat. When you add maple syrup to bread, the loaf isn't as sweet as one made with sugar or honey, but it has a more complex flavor. The coffee creates a pleasing bitterness in the bread that is perfect if you enjoy roast beef or Gruyère sandwiches.

Makes: 1 (2-pound/908 g) loaf (8 slices)	Prep time: 10 minutes	Total time: 3 hours 25 minutes

1 cup (225 to 235 g) whole wheat sourdough starter, fed, active, and at room temperature

1 cup (240 ml) brewed strong coffee (100°F to 110°F, or 38°C to 43°C)

3 tablespoons (60 g) maple syrup

2 tablespoons (30 ml) canola oil

1 teaspoon sea salt

2 cups (250 g) white bread flour

1½ cups (188 g) whole wheat flour

1½ teaspoons instant dry yeast or bread machine yeast

1. Place the starter, coffee, maple syrup, oil, and sea salt in the bread machine's bucket, stirring slightly to combine. Add the white flour, whole wheat flour, and yeast. Program the machine for Sweet/Medium Crust and press Start.

2. When the kneading cycles are complete, remove the paddles, reform the dough, and place it back in the bucket. Let the program continue until it is complete.

3. Cool the bread for 10 minutes, then remove it from the bucket and cool.

4. Store the bread in a sealed plastic bag at room temperature for up to 2 days, or freeze it in a sealed freezer bag with the air pressed out for up to 2 months.

COCONUT WHITE CHOCOLATE BREAD

I am a fan of tropical-themed baked products, and my son is equally enthusiastic about white chocolate. So I combined the two in this dessert-style loaf on a whim, and the results are spectacular. Try a handful of dried cranberries to add a pretty pop of color and burst of tartness.

Makes: 1 (2-pound/908 g) loaf (8 slices)	Prep time: 10 minutes	Total time: 3 hours 25 minutes

1 cup (225 to 235 g) white sourdough starter, fed, active, and at room temperature

1 cup (240 ml) canned coconut milk (100°F to 110°F, or 38°C to 43°C)

2 tablespoons (30 g) packed brown sugar

2 tablespoons (30 ml) melted coconut oil

1¼ teaspoons sea salt

4 cups (480 g) white bread flour

1½ teaspoons instant dry yeast or bread machine yeast

¾ cup (131 g) chopped white chocolate

1. Place the starter, coconut milk, brown sugar, coconut oil, and sea salt in the bread machine's bucket, stirring slightly to combine. Add the flour and yeast. Program the machine for Sweet/Medium Crust and press Start.

2. When the machine signals or the first kneading cycle is complete, add the white chocolate.

3. When the kneading cycles are complete, remove the paddles, reform the dough, and place it back in the bucket. Let the program continue until it is complete.

4. Cool the bread for 10 minutes, then remove it from the bucket and cool.

5. Store the bread in a sealed plastic bag at room temperature for up to 2 days, or freeze it in a sealed freezer bag with the air pressed out for up to 2 months.

HAWAIIAN SOURDOUGH BREAD

The inspiration for this recipe is the soft, fluffy rolls found in Hawaii. I do not use coconut in this loaf, but you can taste the pineapple and ginger in every bite. You can use the medium crust setting if you like a dark crust, but do not use dark because the sugar in the pineapple juice caramelizes very quickly.

Makes: 1 (2-pound/908 g) loaf (8 slices)	Prep time: 10 minutes	Total time: 3 hours 25 minutes

1 cup (225 to 235 g) white sourdough starter, fed, active, and at room temperature

½ cup (120 ml) pineapple juice

½ cup (120 ml) milk (100°F to 110°F, or 38°C to 43°C)

1 large egg, at room temperature, beaten

2 tablespoons (26 g) granulated sugar

2 tablespoons (30 ml) melted butter

1 teaspoon fresh ginger purée

1¼ teaspoons sea salt

4 cups (480 g) white bread flour

1½ teaspoons instant dry yeast or bread machine yeast

1. Place the starter, pineapple juice, milk, egg, sugar, butter, ginger, and sea salt in the bread machine's bucket, stirring slightly to combine. Add the flour and yeast. Program the machine for Sweet/Light Crust and press Start.

2. When the kneading cycles are complete, remove the paddles, reform the dough, and place it back in the bucket. Let the program continue until it is complete.

3. Cool the bread for 10 minutes, then remove it from the bucket and cool.

4. Store the bread in a sealed plastic bag at room temperature for up to 2 days, or freeze it in a sealed freezer bag with the air pressed out for up to 2 months.

SOURDOUGH BARMBRACK

Barmbrack is not as sweet as the other breads in this chapter, but the dried fruit and warm spices create a festive loaf that seems perfect for a treat. This bread is the one I can't resist when it comes out of the bread machine; I bite into a slice long before it has cooled. Try this with sliced chicken and Swiss cheese or toasted with almond butter for a filling lunch.

Makes: 1 (2-pound/908 g) loaf (8 slices)	Prep time: 10 minutes	Total time: 3 hours 25 minutes

1 cup (225 to 235 g) white sourdough starter, fed, active, and at room temperature

1 cup (240 ml) water (100°F to 110°F, or 38°C to 43°C)

3 tablespoons (45 ml) melted butter, cooled

2 tablespoons (26 g) granulated sugar

¾ teaspoon ground cinnamon

¼ teaspoon ground nutmeg

1/2 teaspoon sea salt

4 cups (480 g) white bread flour

1½ teaspoons instant dry yeast or bread machine yeast

1½ cups (225 g) currants or raisins

1. Place the starter, water, butter, sugar, cinnamon, nutmeg, and sea salt in the bread machine's bucket, stirring slightly to combine. Add the flour and yeast. Program the machine for White/Medium Crust and press Start.

2. When the machine signals or the first kneading cycle is complete, add the currants.

3. When the kneading cycles are complete, remove the paddles, reform the dough, and place it back in the bucket. Let the program continue until it is complete.

4. Cool the bread for 10 minutes, then remove it from the bucket and cool.

5. Store the bread in a sealed plastic bag at room temperature for up to 2 days, or freeze it in a sealed freezer bag with the air pressed out for up to 2 months.

GINGERBREAD SOURDOUGH

My nana loved gingerbread in all its forms and made lovely spice-accented buns to serve with Christmas dinner. This bread pays homage to that family recipe. The molasses enhances the fresh ginger and creates darker bread than is expected with white bread flour loaves.

Makes: 1 (2-pound/908 g) loaf (8 slices)	Prep time: 10 minutes	Total time: 3 hours 25 minutes

1 cup (225 to 235 g) white sourdough starter, fed, active, and at room temperature

1 cup (240 ml) water (100°F to 110°F, or 38°C to 43°C)

3 tablespoons (45 ml) melted butter, cooled

2 tablespoons (30 g) packed brown sugar

2 tablespoons (40 g) molasses

2 tablespoons (16 g) skim milk powder

1 tablespoon (6 g) fresh ginger purée

1¼ teaspoons sea salt

4 cups (480 g) white bread flour

1½ teaspoons instant dry yeast or bread machine yeast

1. Place the starter, water, butter, brown sugar, molasses, skim milk powder, ginger, and sea salt in the bread machine's bucket, stirring slightly to combine. Add the flour and yeast. Program the machine for Sweet/Medium Crust and press Start.

2. When the kneading cycles are complete, remove the paddles, reform the dough, and place it back in the bucket. Let the program continue until it is complete.

3. Cool the bread for 10 minutes, then remove it from the bucket and cool.

4. Store the bread in a sealed plastic bag at room temperature for up to 2 days, or freeze it in a sealed freezer bag with the air pressed out for up to 2 months.

SOURDOUGH STOLLEN

Stollen (Weihnachtsstollen) is a German cake-like bread served at Christmastime. This version is very close to baking in the oven, especially if you add the snowy confectioners' sugar glaze. Don't skip the soaking step for the dried fruit, or the flavor and texture will not be perfect.

Makes: 1 (2-pound/908 g) loaf (8 slices)	Prep time: 10 minutes	Total time: 3 hours 25 minutes

1 cup (140 to 150 g) dried fruit or peel (raisins, peel, currants)

1 cup (225 to 235 g) white sourdough starter, fed, active, and at room temperature

1 cup (240 ml) milk (100°F to 110°F, or 38°C to 43°C)

2 tablespoons (26 g) granulated sugar

1 teaspoon sea salt

4 cups (480 g) white bread flour

1½ teaspoons instant dry yeast or bread machine yeast

½ cup (112 g) butter, at room temperature, cut into small chunks

2 tablespoons (30 ml) melted butter

Confectioners' sugar, for dusting

1. Place the dried fruit in a small bowl and cover with hot water and a splash of rum. Set aside for 30 minutes. Drain.

2. Place the starter, milk, sugar, and sea salt in the bread machine's bucket, stirring slightly to combine. Add the flour and yeast. Program the machine for Sweet/Medium Crust and press Start.

3. When the machine signals or the first kneading cycle is complete, add the dried fruit and butter in chunks until incorporated.

4. When the kneading cycles are complete, remove the paddles, reform the dough, and place it back in the bucket. Let the program continue until it is complete.

5. Cool the bread for 10 minutes, remove it from the bucket, brush the loaf with melted butter, and sprinkle generously with confectioners' sugar. Cool completely.

6. Store the bread in a sealed plastic bag at room temperature for up to 2 days, or freeze it in a sealed freezer bag with the air pressed out for up to 2 months.

CHAPTER SEVEN

Breads Flavored with Herbs, Spices, Cheeses, and More

One of my weaknesses is garlic cheese bread, so imagine my delight when I realized I could add those flavors directly to the loaf! This chapter plays with assertive flavors including cheeses, dark chocolate, fresh herbs, pungent spices, and even fresh hot peppers. Be careful with the measurements of these enhancing ingredients, as adding too much can impede the rise or create a soggy texture.

GARLIC PARMESAN SOURDOUGH BREAD

This simple loaf is what I serve with pasta dishes in my home. It is like all-in-one garlic bread that only needs a little butter to make it perfect. You can use grated Parmesan instead of fresh shredded, but the latter seems to have a more assertive flavor.

Makes: 1 (2-pound/908 g) loaf (8 slices)	Prep time: 10 minutes	Total time: 3 hours 25 minutes

1 cup (240 ml) water (100°F to 110°F, or 38°C to 43°C)

¾ cup (168 to 177 g) white sourdough starter, fed, active, and at room temperature

1 tablespoon (15 ml) olive oil

1 tablespoon (10 g) minced garlic

1 teaspoon dried oregano

1 teaspoon sea salt

2½ cups (300 g) white bread flour

1½ cups (188 g) whole wheat flour

1¼ teaspoons instant dry yeast or bread machine yeast

½ cup (40 g) shredded Parmesan cheese

1. Place the water, starter, oil, minced garlic, oregano, and sea salt in the bread machine's bucket, stirring slightly to combine. Add the white bread flour, whole wheat flour, and yeast. Program the machine for Whole Wheat/Medium Crust and press Start.

2. When the machine signals or the first kneading cycle is complete, add the cheese.

3. When the kneading cycles are complete, remove the paddles, reform the dough, and place it back in the bucket. Let the program continue until it is complete.

4. Cool the bread for 10 minutes, then remove it from the bucket and cool.

5. Store the bread in a sealed plastic bag at room temperature for up to 2 days, or freeze it in a sealed freezer bag with the air pressed out for up to 2 months.

BLUE CHEESE PECAN SOURDOUGH

Blue cheese and pecans are a classic pairing in salads, desserts, and appetizers for a good reason: they taste delicious together! I did not specify a type of blue cheese because you might have a favorite, such as Stilton or Roquefort. Stay away from the softer cheeses like Gorgonzola because they change the texture of the bread.

Makes: 1 (2-pound/908 g) loaf (8 slices)	Prep time: 10 minutes	Total time: 3 hours 25 minutes

1¼ cups (281 to 294 g) white sourdough starter, fed, active, and at room temperature

1 cup (240 ml) water (100°F to 110°F, or 38°C to 43°C)

1 tablespoon (15 ml) canola oil

1 tablespoon (20 g) honey

1 teaspoon sea salt

4 cups (480 g) white bread flour

1¼ teaspoons instant dry yeast or bread machine yeast

½ cup (60 g) crumbled blue cheese

½ cup (56 g) chopped pecans

1. Place the starter, water, oil, honey, and sea salt in the bread machine's bucket, stirring slightly to combine. Add the flour and yeast. Program the machine for White/Medium Crust and press Start.

2. When the machine signals or the first kneading cycle is complete, add the cheese and pecans.

3. When the kneading cycles are complete, remove the paddles, reform the dough, and place it back in the bucket. Let the program continue until it is complete.

4. Cool the bread for 10 minutes, then remove it from the bucket and cool.

5. Store the bread in a sealed plastic bag at room temperature for up to 2 days, or freeze it in a sealed freezer bag with the air pressed out for up to 2 months.

SOURDOUGH BEER BREAD

Using beer in sourdough bread enhances that signature tangy flavor and can mimic an older sourdough starter if yours is new. Any type of beer works here, although the darker the beverage, the deeper the taste. I like a lovely stout or German Weisse beer to create a distinctive loaf, and I often add Gruyère or old Cheddar to the dough for a treat.

Makes: 1 (2-pound/908 g) loaf (8 slices)	Prep time: 10 minutes	Total time: 3 hours 25 minutes

1½ cups (337 to 353 g) white sourdough starter, fed, active, and at room temperature

1 cup (240 ml) flat beer (80°F to 90°F, or 27°C to 32°C)

2 tablespoons (30 ml) olive oil

1 tablespoon (20 g) honey

1½ teaspoons sea salt

4 cups (480 g) white bread flour

1 teaspoon quick active dry yeast

1. Place the starter, beer, oil, honey, and sea salt in the bread machine's bucket, stirring slightly to combine. Add the flour and yeast. Program the machine for Basic/Light or Medium Crust and press Start.

2. When the kneading cycles are complete, remove the paddles, reform the dough, and place it back in the bucket. Let the program continue until it is complete.

3. Let the loaf cool for 10 minutes, then turn it out onto a rack to cool.

4. Store the bread in a sealed plastic bag in the refrigerator for up to 4 days, or freeze it in a sealed freezer bag with the air pressed out for up to 2 months.

BITTER DARK CHOCOLATE SOURDOUGH

Cocoa powder is not sweet; its complex flavor and dark color usually create a savory loaf. I added extra sugar and vanilla extract to mellow the bread and used all white flour to distinguish this bread from pumpernickel. If you enjoy bread pudding, try this loaf in your favorite recipe.

Makes: 1 (2-pound/908 g) loaf (8 slices)	Prep time: 10 minutes	Total time: 3 hours 25 minutes

1 cup (225 to 235 g) white sourdough starter, fed, active, and at room temperature

1 cup (240 ml) water (100°F to 110°F, or 38°C to 43°C)

¼ cup (22 g) unsweetened cocoa powder

2 tablespoons (30 ml) melted butter, cooled

2 tablespoons (30 g) packed brown sugar

1 teaspoon pure vanilla extract

1 teaspoon sea salt

3½ cups (420 g) white bread flour

1½ teaspoons instant dry yeast or bread machine yeast

¾ cup (131 g) dark chocolate chips

1. Place the starter, water, cocoa powder, butter, brown sugar, vanilla, and sea salt in the bread machine's bucket, stirring slightly to combine. Add the flour and yeast. Program the machine for Sweet/Medium Crust and press Start.

2. When the machine signals or the first kneading cycle is complete, add the chocolate chips.

3. When the kneading cycles are complete, remove the paddles, reform the dough, and place it back in the bucket. Let the program continue until it is complete.

4. Cool the bread for 10 minutes, then remove it from the bucket and cool.

5. Store the bread in a sealed plastic bag at room temperature for up to 2 days, or freeze it in a sealed freezer bag with the air pressed out for up to 2 months.

ROSEMARY SOURDOUGH

Rosemary was never my first choice of culinary herbs until I put it in bread. This is a potent herb, so don't exceed the amount in the recipe unless you love the taste. You can substitute thyme if rosemary is not available or you don't fancy it.

Makes: 1 (2-pound/908 g) loaf (8 slices)	Prep time: 10 minutes	Total time: 3 hours 25 minutes

1¼ cups (295 ml) water (100°F to 110°F, or 38°C to 43°C)

¾ cup (168 to 177 g) white sourdough starter, fed, active, and at room temperature

1½ tablespoons (3 g) finely chopped fresh rosemary leaves

2 tablespoons (30 ml) olive oil

1½ teaspoons sea salt

3½ cups (420 g) white bread flour

1¼ teaspoons instant dry yeast or bread machine yeast

1. Place the water, starter, rosemary, oil, and sea salt in the bread machine's bucket, stirring slightly to combine. Add the flour and yeast. Program the machine for White/Medium Crust and press Start.

2. When the kneading cycles are complete, remove the paddles, reform the dough, and place it back in the bucket. Let the program continue until it is complete.

3. Cool the bread for 10 minutes, then remove it from the bucket and cool.

4. Store the bread in a sealed plastic bag at room temperature for up to 2 days, or freeze it in a sealed freezer bag with the air pressed out for up to 2 months.

SOURDOUGH GRUYÈRE BREAD

Gruyère is a nutty, sweetish Swiss cheese without the characteristic holes. Depending on its age, the flavor will be mild or intense. This loaf is terrific for ham sandwiches, or if you are feeling experimental, add 1 cup (150 g) of chopped ham to the loaf after the first kneading cycle.

Makes: 1 (2-pound/908 g) loaf (8 slices)	Prep time: 10 minutes	Total time: 3 hours 25 minutes

1 cup (225 to 235 g) white sourdough starter, active, and at room temperature

¾ cup (175 ml) water (100°F to 110°F, or 38°C to 43°C)

1 tablespoon (13 g) granulated sugar

1 tablespoon (15 ml) olive oil

1¼ teaspoons sea salt

½ teaspoon ground nutmeg

2½ cups (300 g) white bread flour

1 cup (125 g) whole wheat flour

1¼ teaspoons instant dry yeast or bread machine yeast

1 cup (120 g) shredded Gruyère cheese

1. Place the starter, water, sugar, oil, sea salt, and nutmeg in the bread machine's bucket, stirring slightly to combine. Add the white bread flour, whole wheat flour, and yeast. Program the machine for Whole Wheat/Medium Crust and press Start.

2. When the machine signals or the first kneading cycle is complete, add the cheese.

3. When the kneading cycles are complete, remove the paddles, reform the dough, and place it back in the bucket. Let the program continue until it is complete.

4. Cool the bread for 10 minutes, then remove it from the bucket and cool.

5. Store the bread in a sealed plastic bag at room temperature for up to 2 days, or freeze it in a sealed freezer bag with the air pressed out for up to 2 months.

SOURDOUGH PUMPERNICKEL

I have an addiction to bread—I love it all—but pumpernickel is hands down my favorite. The color, taste, and texture work for sandwiches, dips, and as an edible bowl for soups and stews. This loaf can be baked in the oven, as well, if you follow the same rising, shaping, and baking instructions as the San Francisco Sourdough (page 166).

Makes: 1 (2-pound/908 g) loaf (8 slices)	Prep time: 10 minutes	Total time: 3 hours 25 minutes

1 cup (225 to 235 g) white sourdough starter, fed, active, and at room temperature

½ cup (120 ml) strong brewed coffee (100°F to 110°F, or 38°C to 43°C)

3 tablespoons (60 g) blackstrap molasses

2 tablespoons (30 ml) melted butter, cooled

1½ tablespoons (8 g) unsweetened cocoa powder

1¼ teaspoons sea salt

2½ cups (320 g) dark rye flour

1 cup (125 g) whole wheat flour

1½ teaspoons instant dry yeast or bread machine yeast

1. Place the starter, coffee, molasses, butter, cocoa powder, and sea salt in the bread machine's bucket, stirring slightly to combine. Add the rye flour, whole wheat flour, and yeast. Program the machine for White/Medium Crust and press Start.

2. When the kneading cycles are complete, remove the paddles, reform the dough, and place it back in the bucket. Let the program continue until it is complete.

3. Cool the bread for 10 minutes, then remove it from the bucket and cool.

4. Store the bread in a sealed plastic bag at room temperature for up to 2 days, or freeze it in a sealed freezer bag with the air pressed out for up to 2 months.

PESTO SOURDOUGH BREAD

This is similar to Pine Nut Basil Sourdough (page 85) but uses sundried tomato pesto instead and omits the nuts. You can make your own pesto but store-bought tastes delicious. I like this bread toasted with thick slices of Havarti or Gouda.

Makes: 1 (2-pound/908 g) loaf (8 slices)	Prep time: 10 minutes	Total time: 3 hours 25 minutes

1¼ cups (281 to 294 g) white sourdough starter, fed, active, and at room temperature

1 cup (240 ml) water (100°F to 110°F, or 38°C to 43°C)

¼ cup (65 g) store-bought sundried tomato pesto

1½ tablespoons (20 g) granulated sugar

1¼ teaspoons sea salt

4 cups (480 g) white bread flour

1¼ teaspoons instant dry yeast or bread machine yeast

1. Place the starter, water, pesto, sugar, and sea salt in the bread machine's bucket, stirring slightly to combine. Add the flour and yeast. Program the machine for White/Medium Crust and press Start.

2. When the kneading cycles are complete, remove the paddles, reform the dough, and place it back in the bucket. Let the program continue until it is complete.

3. Cool the bread for 10 minutes, then remove it from the bucket and cool.

4. Store the bread in a sealed plastic bag at room temperature for up to 2 days, or freeze it in a sealed freezer bag with the air pressed out for up to 2 months.

JALAPEÑO OLD CHEDDAR SOURDOUGH BREAD

Every bite of this bread bursts with Southwest flavor, even with just ¼ cup (36 g) of chopped jalapeños. The best part is that the Cheddar in the dough crisps up golden and salty on the exposed crust. Cut a couple slices for a gourmet grilled cheese sandwich.

Makes: 1 (2-pound/908 g) loaf (8 slices)	Prep time: 10 minutes	Total time: 3 hours 25 minutes

1 cup (225 to 235 g) white sourdough starter, fed, active, and at room temperature

1 cup (240 ml) water (100°F to 110°F, or 38°C to 43°C)

1 teaspoon sea salt

2¾ cups (340 g) white bread flour

1 cup (125 g) whole wheat flour

1¼ teaspoons instant dry yeast or bread machine yeast

¾ cup (80 g) shredded old Cheddar

¼ cup (36 g) chopped pickled jalapeño peppers

1. Place the starter, water, and sea salt in the bread machine's bucket, stirring slightly to combine. Add the white bread flour, whole wheat flour, and yeast. Program the machine for Whole Wheat/Medium Crust and press Start.

2. When the machine signals or the first kneading cycle is complete, add the cheese and jalapeño.

3. When the kneading cycles are complete, remove the paddles, reform the dough, and place it back in the bucket. Let the program continue until it is complete.

4. Cool the bread for 10 minutes, then remove it from the bucket and cool.

5. Store the bread in a sealed plastic bag at room temperature for up to 2 days, or freeze it in a sealed freezer bag with the air pressed out for up to 2 months.

CHEESY BACON SOURDOUGH

My husband asks for this bread whenever I give him a choice because, you know, bacon! If you cook the slices very crispy, they will not break down as much in the kneading process. I sometimes add pancetta instead of bacon for a more intense flavor.

Makes: 1 (2-pound/908 g) loaf (8 slices)	Prep time: 10 minutes	Total time: 3 hours 25 minutes

1 cup (225 to 235 g) white sourdough starter, fed, active, and at room temperature

¾ cup (175 ml) water (100°F to 110°F, or 38°C to 43°C)

1 tablespoon (15 ml) melted butter, cooled

1 tablespoon (13 g) granulated sugar

1 teaspoon sea salt

3½ cups (420 g) white bread flour

1½ teaspoons instant dry yeast or bread machine yeast

½ cup (40 g) chopped cooked bacon

½ cup (58 g) shredded Cheddar

1. Place the starter, water, butter, sugar, and sea salt in the bread machine's bucket, stirring slightly to combine. Add the flour and yeast. Program the machine for White/Medium Crust and press Start.

2. When the machine signals or the first kneading cycle is complete, add the bacon and Cheddar.

3. When the kneading cycles are complete, remove the paddles, reform the dough, and place it back in the bucket. Let the program continue until it is complete.

4. Cool the bread for 10 minutes, then remove it from the bucket and cool.

5. Store the bread in a sealed plastic bag at room temperature for up to 2 days, or freeze it in a sealed freezer bag with the air pressed out for up to 2 months.

THYME HONEY SOURDOUGH BREAD

Thyme took over my garden about two years ago, spilling into my perennials and over the rocks that mark the borders. I try to incorporate this plethora of herbs in many dishes and baked items such as this loaf. Honey enhances the slightly floral character of the bread.

Makes: 1 (2-pound/908 g) loaf (8 slices)	Prep time: 10 minutes	Total time: 3 hours 25 minutes

1 cup (225 to 235 g) white sourdough starter, fed, active, and at room temperature

1¼ cups (295 ml) water (100°F to 110°F, or 38°C to 43°C)

2 tablespoons (40 g) honey

1½ tablespoons (25 ml) canola oil

2 teaspoons (2 g) chopped fresh thyme

1¼ teaspoons sea salt

3 cups (360 g) white bread flour

1 cup (128 g) light rye flour

1¼ teaspoons instant dry yeast or bread machine yeast

1. Place the starter, water, honey, oil, thyme, and sea salt in the bread machine's bucket, stirring slightly to combine. Add the white bread flour, rye flour, and yeast. Program the machine for White/Medium Crust and press Start.

2. When the kneading cycles are complete, remove the paddles, reform the dough, and place it back in the bucket. Let the program continue until it is complete.

3. Cool the bread for 10 minutes, then remove it from the bucket and cool.

4. Store the bread in a sealed plastic bag at room temperature for up to 2 days, or freeze it in a sealed freezer bag with the air pressed out for up to 2 months.

DILL SOURDOUGH

This is a crusty golden loaf with a fluffy, fine-crumbed interior scented with dill. I make this bread when we crave salmon salad sandwiches or toast it and top with cream cheese and smoked salmon. Dried dill does not have as intense flavor as fresh but can be used if you reduce the amount to 1½ teaspoons.

Makes: 1 (2-pound/908 g) loaf (8 slices)	Prep time: 10 minutes	Total time: 3 hours 25 minutes

1 cup (225 to 235 g) white sourdough starter, fed, active, and at room temperature

¾ cup (175 ml) water (100°F to 110°F, or 38°C to 43°C)

2 tablespoons (26 g) granulated sugar

1 tablespoon (15 ml) canola oil

1 tablespoon (4 g) chopped fresh dill

1¼ teaspoons sea salt

3½ cups (420 g) white bread flour

1 teaspoon instant dry yeast or bread machine yeast

1. Place the starter, water, sugar, oil, dill, and sea salt in the bread machine's bucket, stirring slightly to combine. Add the flour and yeast. Program the machine for White/Medium Crust and press Start.

2. When the kneading cycles are complete, remove the paddles, reform the dough, and place it back in the bucket. Let the program continue until it is complete.

3. Cool the bread for 10 minutes, then remove it from the bucket and cool.

4. Store the bread in a sealed plastic bag at room temperature for up to 2 days, or freeze it in a sealed freezer bag with the air pressed out for up to 2 months.

MOLASSES GINGER SOURDOUGH

Molasses is an underutilized sweetener, which is a shame because it has a delightful flavor accented here with fresh ginger. If you can't find fresh ginger purée, use 1½ teaspoons of ground ginger instead. This loaf is sublime with a thick layer of apple butter.

Makes: 1 (2-pound/908 g) loaf (8 slices)	Prep time: 10 minutes	Total time: 3 hours 25 minutes

1 cup (225 to 235 g) white sourdough starter, fed, active, and at room temperature

¾ cup (175 ml) milk (100°F to 110°F, or 38°C to 43°C)

¼ cup (80 g) blackstrap molasses

3 tablespoons (45 ml) melted butter, cooled

1 tablespoon (6 g) fresh ginger purée

1 teaspoon sea salt

3¾ cups (450 g) white bread flour

1¼ teaspoons instant dry yeast or bread machine yeast

1. Place the starter, milk, molasses, butter, ginger, and sea salt in the bread machine's bucket, stirring slightly to combine. Add the flour and yeast. Program the machine for White/Medium Crust and press Start.

2. When the kneading cycles are complete, remove the paddles, reform the dough, and place it back in the bucket. Let the program continue until it is complete.

3. Cool the bread for 10 minutes, then remove it from the bucket and cool.

4. Store the bread in a sealed plastic bag at room temperature for up to 2 days, or freeze it in a sealed freezer bag with the air pressed out for up to 2 months.

ESPRESSO SOURDOUGH BREAD

Despite its name, this loaf does not have a strong coffee taste; the bread has a complex flavor with a hint of cinnamon. If you can't brew espresso, you can replace it with water and 2 teaspoons of instant coffee. Cut a few slices to serve with stew or hearty chowders.

Makes: 1 (2-pound/908 g) loaf (8 slices)	Prep time: 10 minutes	Total time: 3 hours 25 minutes

1 cup (225 to 235 g) white sourdough starter, fed, active, and at room temperature

½ cup (120 ml) water (100°F to 110°F, or 38°C to 43°C)

½ cup (120 ml) freshly brewed espresso (100°F to 110°F, or 38°C to 43°C)

1½ teaspoons granulated sugar

1 teaspoon sea salt

½ teaspoon ground cinnamon

2½ cups (300 g) white bread flour

1 cup (125 g) whole wheat flour

1 teaspoon instant dry yeast or bread machine yeast

1. Place the starter, water, espresso, sugar, sea salt, and cinnamon in the bread machine's bucket, stirring slightly to combine. Add the white bread flour, whole wheat flour, and yeast. Program the machine for Whole Wheat/Medium Crust and press Start.

2. When the kneading cycles are complete, remove the paddles, reform the dough, and place it back in the bucket. Let the program continue until it is complete.

3. Cool the bread for 10 minutes, then remove it from the bucket and cool.

4. Store the bread in a sealed plastic bag at room temperature for up to 2 days, or freeze it in a sealed freezer bag with the air pressed out for up to 2 months.

TOMATO FETA SOURDOUGH

This savory loaf is reddish in color with small white pockets of salty cheese. The added basil and garlic create a distinctly Mediterranean character that is delicious with no embellishment. You can also try hard goat cheese in place of the feta.

Makes: 1 (2-pound/908 g) loaf (8 slices)	Prep time: 10 minutes	Total time: 3 hours 25 minutes

1 cup (225 to 235 g) white sourdough starter, fed, active, and at room temperature

1 cup (240 ml) water (100°F to 110°F, or 38°C to 43°C)

½ cup (130 g) tomato paste

1 tablespoon (15 ml) olive oil

2 teaspoons (6 g) minced garlic

1 teaspoon dried basil

1 teaspoon sea salt

4 cups (480 g) white bread flour

1¼ teaspoons instant dry yeast or bread machine yeast

¾ cup (168 g) crumbled feta cheese

1. Place the starter, water, tomato paste, oil, garlic, basil, and sea salt in the bread machine's bucket, stirring slightly to combine. Add the flour and yeast. Program the machine for White/Medium Crust and press Start.

2. When the machine signals or the first kneading cycle is complete, add the feta.

3. When the kneading cycles are complete, remove the paddles, reform the dough, and place it back in the bucket. Let the program continue until it is complete.

4. Cool the bread for 10 minutes, then remove it from the bucket and cool.

5. Store the bread in a sealed plastic bag at room temperature for up to 2 days, or freeze it in a sealed freezer bag with the air pressed out for up to 2 months.

CHAPTER EIGHT

Shaped Breads and Buns

The breads in this chapter are completed in the oven, and their shapes and finishes will resemble familiar oval loaves and buns. Before you get started, read through your chosen recipe to make sure you allocate enough time for the shaping and second rise. Also make sure you have any extra equipment, such as loaf pans or baking sheets. The dough is made in the bread machine, so the hard work of kneading and the first rise will be done for you. After shaping your first loaf or bun, the technique will become second nature; don't be surprised if you start to experiment with different shapes. Have fun!

SOURDOUGH BAGUETTES

When I worked in North Africa, the bakeries created the most incredible baguettes in massive clay or brick ovens. I would often pick up a half dozen piping-hot loaves on the way home and finish one off in the car. The method might seem labor-intensive, but the results are worth it.

Makes: 2 loaves	Prep time: 30 minutes	Cook time: 25 minutes Rise time: Dough program, plus 1 hour

1½ cups (337 to 353 g) white sourdough starter, fed, active, and at room temperature

1½ cups (355 ml) water (100°F to 110°F, or 38°C to 43°C)

1 tablespoon (20 g) honey

2 teaspoons (10 ml) olive oil

1½ teaspoons sea salt

4 cups (480 g) white bread flour

1½ teaspoons instant dry yeast or bread machine yeast

1. Place the starter, water, honey, oil, and sea salt in the bread machine's bucket, stirring slightly to combine. Add the flour and yeast. Program the machine for Dough and press Start.

2. When the dough cycle is complete, transfer the dough to a lightly floured surface. Cut the dough into 2 equal pieces, roll them into balls, and set one aside covered with a clean cloth.

3. Roll the remaining piece into a rectangle about ½ inch (1 cm) thick. Fold the edge closest to you into the center and use your fingertips to seal the middle edge. Rotate the dough so the unfolded side is closest, and fold the dough into the center so the edge is right up against the other edge. Seal the edge with your fingertips, then make the center indent deeper.

4. Fold the top edge to one-third of the width, and use the heel of your right hand to seal the edge. Fold the top edge again over the first fold, so it lines up with the center indentation, and seal the edge with the heel of your hand. Now fold the top edge over so the bottom and top edges are lined up and seal the dough to form a smooth cylinder.

5. Place the seal-side down. Starting in the middle of the cylinder, use your palms to roll the baguette gently, pressing to the outsides to elongate it. Continue rolling until you have a 16-inch (41-cm) baguette with tapered ends.

6. Place the baguette dough on a parchment-lined baking sheet and repeat with the remaining piece of dough. Cover the baguettes with lightly oiled plastic wrap and set aside until doubled, about 1 hour.

7. Preheat the oven to 450°F (230°C, or gas mark 8) and place a baking dish on the bottom rack. Make four diagonal slashes in each baguette with a sharp knife and place them in the oven. Add 5 or 6 ice cubes to the baking dish and bake the baguettes until they are deep golden brown, about 25 minutes.

8. Remove the baguettes from the oven and place onto a rack to cool.

9. Store the bread in a sealed plastic bag at room temperature for 1 day, or freeze in a sealed freezer bag with the air pressed out for up to 2 months.

SAN FRANCISCO SOURDOUGH BREAD

The sourdough starter I use currently is from a San Francisco batch dating back 150 years; I ordered it for its incredible flavor and lovely active yeast. This recipe is chewy, thick-crusted, and a little denser from the addition of whole wheat flour.

Makes: 2 loaves	Prep time: 30 minutes	Cook time: 30 minutes Rise time: Dough program, plus 2 hours

1¼ cups (281– to 294 g) white sourdough starter, fed, active, and at room temperature

½ cup (120 ml) water (100°F to 110°F, or 38°C to 43°C)

½ cup (120 ml) milk (100°F to 110°F, or 38°C to 43°C)

2½ tablespoons (40 ml) olive oil

1½ tablespoons (20 g) granulated sugar

1½ teaspoons sea salt

3½ cups (420 g) white bread flour

½ cup (64 g) whole wheat flour

1½ teaspoons bread machine or quick active dry yeast

1. Place the starter, water, milk, oil, sugar, and sea salt in the bread machine's bucket, stirring slightly to combine. Add the white bread flour, whole wheat flour, and yeast. Program the machine for Dough and press Start.

2. When the dough cycle is complete, transfer the dough to a lightly floured work surface. Separate the dough into 2 equal pieces.

3. Form one piece into an oval, then cup your hands around the sides and drag it toward you to create tension on the surface.

4. Rotate the ball a complete turn and drag it again. Continue the process until the dough is a smooth oval and the surface is taut.

5. Transfer the dough to a parchment-lined baking sheet, and repeat with the remaining dough. Cover the loaves with lightly oiled plastic wrap and set them aside until doubled, about 2 hours.

6. Preheat the oven to 400°F (200°C, or gas mark 6). Make three ¼-inch (6-mm)-deep diagonal slashes in the top of the loaves and bake them until golden brown, about 30 minutes.

7. Place the bread onto a rack to cool and serve.

8. Store the bread in a sealed plastic bag at room temperature for up to 3 days, or freeze in a sealed freezer bag with the air pressed out for up to 2 months.

SOURDOUGH HERB SWIRL BREAD

There is something charming about revealing a swirl in the middle of a golden loaf when you cut it. The swirl here is composed of several flavorful herbs and smells spectacular.

Makes: 1 loaf	Prep time: 30 minutes	Cook time: 30 minutes Rise time: Dough program, plus 2 hours

1 cup (225 to 235 g) white sourdough starter, fed, active, and at room temperature

½ cup (120 ml) water (100°F to 110°F, or 38°C to 43°C)

2 tablespoons (26 g) granulated sugar

2 tablespoons (30 ml) canola oil

1 teaspoon sea salt

3 cups (360 g) white bread flour

1¼ teaspoons instant dry yeast or bread machine yeast

1 tablespoon (3 g) dried oregano

1 tablespoon (5 g) dried basil

2 teaspoons (1 g) dried thyme

1. Place the starter, water, sugar, oil, and sea salt in the bread machine's bucket, stirring slightly to combine. Add the flour and yeast. Program the machine for Dough and press Start.

2. When the dough cycle is complete, transfer the dough to a lightly oiled bowl, turning to coat, and cover with a clean kitchen cloth. Set the dough aside to double, about 1 hour.

3. Transfer the dough to a floured work surface and roll it into a 12- x 8-inch (30- x 20-cm) rectangle. Sprinkle the herbs evenly all over the surface of the dough, leaving a ½-inch (1-cm) border. Roll the dough up tightly jelly-roll style and pinch the edge to seal.

4. Lightly grease a 9- x 5-inch (23- x 13-cm) loaf pan and place the rolled dough seam-side down in the pan. Cover the pan with a clean kitchen towel and set it aside to rise until doubled, about 1 hour.

5. Preheat the oven to 350°F (175°C, or gas mark 4). Bake the bread until golden brown and has an internal temperature of 200°F (93°C) about 30 minutes.

6. Place the bread onto a rack to cool and serve.

7. Store the bread in a sealed plastic bag at room temperature for up to 5 days, or freeze it in a sealed freezer bag with the air pressed out for up to 2 months.

ARTISAN SOURDOUGH BREAD

I love a rustic, irregular loaf, so this recipe is obviously one of my favorites. The shape is called a boule or ball, and this construction is seen in many French loaves. Don't worry if the loaf has a dusting of flour when you bake it; that coating adds to the appearance and makes the slashes in the bread stand out beautifully.

Makes: 1 loaf	Prep time: 20 minutes	Cook time: 30 minutes Rise time: Dough program, plus 2 hours

1¼ cups (281 to 294 g) white sourdough starter, fed, active, and at room temperature

1¼ cups (295 ml) water (100°F to 110°F, or 38°C to 43°C)

1 tablespoon (15 ml) olive oil

1 tablespoon (20 g) honey

2 teaspoons (8 g) sea salt

4 cups (480 g) white bread flour

1¼ teaspoons instant dry yeast

1. Place the starter, water, oil, honey, and sea salt in the bread machine's bucket, stirring slightly to combine. Add the flour and yeast. Program the machine for Dough and press Start.

2. When the dough cycle is complete, remove the dough from the bucket, gather it into a ball, and transfer the dough to a lightly floured work surface.

3. Cup both hands on the far side of the ball and drag it toward you gently, creating tension on the surface. Rotate the ball a half turn and drag it again. Continue the process until the dough is a smooth round and the surface is taut.

4. Transfer the dough to a parchment-lined baking sheet, cover it with lightly oiled plastic wrap, and set it aside to rise until doubled, about 2 hours.

5. Preheat the oven to 400°F (200°C, or gas mark 6). Make two or three diagonal slashes about ¼-inch (6-mm) deep in the top of the loaf and bake until it is golden brown and has an internal temperature of 200°F (93°C) 25 to 30 minutes.

6. Cool the bread and serve.

7. Store the bread in a sealed plastic bag at room temperature for up to 3 days, or freeze it in a sealed freezer bag with the air pressed out for up to 2 months.

SOURDOUGH CIABATTA BREAD

My mom always bought ciabatta in loaf and bun form because she felt the crust was the most important part—the thicker, the better. You can make this recipe in the bread machine, but using the oven and a water pan ensures that signature crust.

Makes: 2 loaves	Prep time: 30 minutes	Cook time: 30 minutes
		Rise time: Dough program, plus 4 hours

¾ cup (168 to 177 g) white sourdough starter, fed, active, and at room temperature

1¼ cups (295 ml) water (100°F to 110°F, or 38°C to 43°C)

2 tablespoons (30 ml) olive oil

1½ teaspoons sea salt

3¼ cups (390 g) white bread flour

1¼ teaspoons instant dry yeast or bread machine yeast

1. Place the starter, water, oil, and sea salt in the bread machine's bucket, stirring slightly to combine. Add the flour and yeast. Program the machine for Dough and press Start.

2. When the dough cycle is complete, transfer the dough to a bowl and cover with a damp, clean kitchen cloth. For every 30 minutes over 2 hours, fold the dough over itself by lifting a side, dragging it over the top, and pressing to seal. Do this with all four sides and cover the bowl.

3. Line a baking sheet with parchment and dust it with cornmeal. Divide the dough into 2 equal pieces and pat one piece into a rectangle. Fold the sides into the middle, overlapping them. Then roll the folded sections into a log.

4. Drag the log toward you gently, then transfer it to the baking sheet. Repeat with the remaining piece. Cover loosely with a clean cloth and set aside until almost doubled, about 2 hours.

5. Preheat the oven to 425°F (220°C, or gas mark 7) and place a baking dish filled with 1 cup (240 ml) of water on the bottom rack. Bake until it is deep brown and has an internal temperature of 200°F (93°C), 25 to 30 minutes.

6. Cool the bread on a rack for at least 1 hour and serve.

7. Store the bread in a sealed plastic bag at room temperature for up to 3 days, or freeze it in a sealed freezer bag for up to 2 months.

CRUSTY SOURDOUGH ROLLS

Buns are one of the easiest shaped breads, and they are so fun to make, you might throw these together every week. If you feel fancy, you can also create knots by rolling your pieces into 8-inch (20-cm) ropes and knotting them in the middle. Tuck the ends under to create a neat appearance; let them rise and bake.

Makes: 8 rolls	Prep time: 30 minutes	Cook time: 18 minutes | Rise time: Dough program, plus 45 minutes

1¼ cups (281–294 g) white sourdough starter, fed, active, and at room temperature

¾ cup (175 ml) water (100°F to 110°F, or 38°C to 43°C)

1 teaspoon granulated sugar

1 teaspoon canola oil

1¼ teaspoons sea salt

2½ cups (300 g) white bread flour

1 teaspoon instant dry yeast or bread machine yeast

1. Place the starter, water, sugar, oil, and sea salt in the bread machine's bucket, stirring slightly to combine. Add the flour and yeast. Program the machine for Dough and press Start.

2. When the dough cycle is complete, transfer the dough to a lightly floured work surface and divide it into 8 equal pieces.

3. Line a baking sheet with parchment paper and dust it with flour or cornmeal. Shape each piece into a ball and create surface tension by cupping your hands around the sides of the ball and drawing downward.

4. Place each bun on the baking sheet, spacing them out evenly. Lightly dust the buns with flour and cover them loosely with a clean kitchen cloth. Set aside to rise for 45 minutes.

5. Preheat the oven to 450°F (230°C, or gas mark 8) and place a baking dish filled with 1 cup (240 ml) of water on the bottom rack. Bake the rolls until they are golden brown, about 18 minutes.

6. Cool the rolls on a rack and serve.

7. Store the buns in a sealed plastic bag in the refrigerator for up to 4 days, or freeze in a sealed freezer bag with the air pressed out for up to 1 month.

SOURDOUGH CINNAMON ROLLS WITH CREAM CHEESE ICING

You might notice this recipe is a little longer and requires a bit more work, but once you try it, you will get the hang of the steps quickly. I sometimes add raisins and nuts to the filling swirl, and if you try that variation, make sure you roll the dough very tightly. They are delightful unglazed, but then you will miss licking the frosting off your fingers when the bun is gone.

Makes: 8 buns	Prep time: 30 minutes	Cook time: 25 minutes
		Rise time: Dough program, plus 3 hours

For the Dough

¾ cup (168 to 177 g) white sourdough starter, fed, active, and at room temperature

¾ cup (175 ml) milk (100°F to 110°F, or 38°C to 43°C)

2 tablespoons (26 g) granulated sugar

2 tablespoons (30 ml) melted butter, cooled

¼ teaspoon sea salt

2 cups (250 g) white bread flour

1¼ teaspoons instant dry yeast or bread machine yeast

For the Filling

¼ cup (60 ml) butter, softened

½ cup (115 g) packed brown sugar

2 teaspoons (5 g) ground cinnamon

1. Place the starter, milk, sugar, melted butter, and sea salt in the bread machine's bucket, stirring slightly to combine. Add the flour and yeast. Program the machine for Dough and press Start.

2. When the dough cycle is complete, transfer the dough to a lightly oiled bowl, turning to coat, and cover with a clean kitchen cloth. Set the dough aside to double, about 2 hours.

3. Lightly butter a 9- x 13-inch (23- x 33-cm) baking dish and set it aside.

4. Transfer the dough to a floured work surface and roll or pat it into a 12- x 8-inch (30- x 20-cm) rectangle. Spread the softened butter evenly over the dough right to the edges.

5. In a small bowl, combine the brown sugar and cinnamon and sprinkle evenly over the melted butter. Roll the dough up tightly jelly-roll style and pinch the edge to seal.

6. Use a sharp knife to cut the roll into 1-inch (2.5-cm)-thick rolls and place them in the baking dish. Cover loosely with a clean kitchen cloth and set aside to double, about 1 hour.

Cream Cheese Icing

½ cup (115 g) cream cheese, at room temperature

¼ cup (55 g) butter, at room temperature

1 to 1½ cups (90 to 120 g) sifted confectioners' sugar

1 teaspoon vanilla extract

7. Preheat the oven to 350°F (175°C, or gas mark 4). Bake until the rolls are golden brown, 20 to 25 minutes.

8. While the rolls are baking, beat the cream cheese and butter together in a small bowl with electric hand beaters. Add the confectioners' sugar and vanilla and beat until creamy and smooth.

9. Remove the buns from the oven and let them cool on a rack for 20 minutes before spreading the icing evenly over them. Serve.

10. Store the rolls in a sealed container in the refrigerator for up to 5 days or in the freezer for up to 1 month.

Roll or pat the dough into a rectangle.

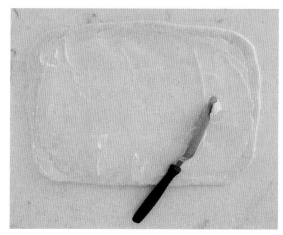

Spread butter evenly over the dough to the edges.

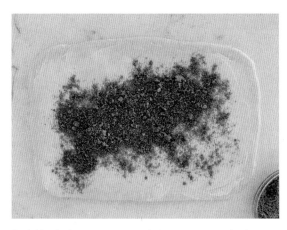

Sprinkle the brown sugar and cinnamon over the butter. Begin rolling up the dough.

Continue rolling until you have a tight cylinder.

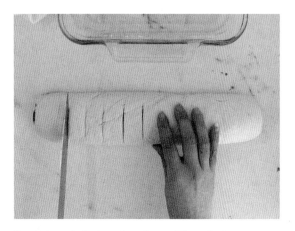

Use a sharp knife to cut sections of the cylinder.

Place the sections in the baking dish.

Cover the dish with a kitchen cloth and set aside.

SOURDOUGH BAGELS

There is an interesting debate about which bagel—Montreal or New York—is the best, and because I am Canadian, I fall on the Montreal side. Despite that affiliation, these bagels are more like the New York version: larger, doughier, and soft exterior. You can sprinkle these with sesame seeds, poppy seeds, or everything bagel spice instead of salt.

Makes: 12 bagels	Prep time: 30 minutes	Cook time: 20 minutes | Rise time: Dough program, plus 4 hours

1¼ cups (281 to 294 g) white sourdough starter, fed, active, and at room temperature

1¼ cups (295 ml) water (100°F to 110°F, or 38°C to 43°C)

1 tablespoon (13 g) granulated sugar

1 tablespoon (15 ml) melted butter, cooled

1½ teaspoons sea salt

4½ cups (540 g) white bread flour

1 teaspoon instant dry yeast or bread machine yeast

2 tablespoons (30 g) baking soda

1 large egg, at room temperature, beaten

2 tablespoons (30 ml) water

Coarse sea salt, for topping

1. Place the starter, water, sugar, butter, and sea salt in the bread machine's bucket, stirring slightly to combine. Add the flour and yeast. Program the machine for Dough and press Start.

2. When the dough cycle is complete, transfer the dough to a lightly greased large bowl. Cover with a clean kitchen cloth and set aside for 3 hours, folding the dough every hour to deflate the dough.

3. Carefully turn the dough out onto a lightly floured surface, trying to keep as much air as possible. Divide the dough into 12 equal pieces and roll each gently into a ball. Create a 1½-inch (3.5-cm) hole in the center of each using your fingertips. Place the bagels on a parchment-lined baking sheet, cover loosely with a clean kitchen towel, and set aside for 1 hour.

4. Preheat the oven to 450°F (230°C, or gas mark 8). Fill a large, deep saucepan three-quarters full of water and stir in the baking soda. Bring the water to a boil over high heat. Drop the bagels into the boiling water, about 2 per batch, and boil for 1 minute, turning at 30 seconds. Transfer the boiled bagels to a second parchment-lined baking sheet with a slotted spoon and repeat with the remaining bagels.

5. In a small bowl, whisk the egg and water until frothy. Brush the tops of the bagels with the mixture and sprinkle them with coarse salt.

6. Bake until golden brown, about 20 minutes.

7. Serve warm or store the cooled bagels in a sealed plastic bag at room temperature for up to 5 days, or freeze in a sealed freezer bag with the air pressed out for up to 2 months.

SOURDOUGH BREADSTICKS

These are the soft type of breadstick, not grissini, which are thinner, crispier, and drier. These are perfect for dipping in bowls of steaming soup or serving alongside tempting dips. If you prefer a slightly crunchier crust, omit the melted butter finish.

Makes: 20 bread sticks	Prep time: 20 minutes	Cook time: 15 minutes | Rise time: Dough program, plus 30 minutes

1¼ cups (281 to 294 g) white sourdough starter, fed, active, and at room temperature

¾ cup (175 ml) water (100°F to 110°F, or 38°C to 43°C)

1½ teaspoons sea salt

3¼ cups (390 g) white bread flour

1¼ teaspoons instant dry yeast or bread machine yeast

2 tablespoons (30 ml) melted butter

1. Place the starter, water, and sea salt in the bread machine's bucket, stirring slightly to combine. Add the flour and yeast. Program the machine for Dough and press Start.

2. When the dough cycle is complete, transfer the dough to a lightly floured work surface.

3. Divide the dough into 20 equal pieces and roll each into a 6- to 8-inch (15- to 20-cm) rope. Place them on two baking sheets about 2 inches (5 cm) apart. Cover the dough loosely with clean kitchen cloths and set aside for 30 minutes to rise.

4. Preheat the oven to 350°F (175°C, or gas mark 4). Bake the breadsticks until golden brown, 12 to 15 minutes.

5. Remove them from the oven, brush generously with the melted butter, and serve warm.

6. Store the cooled breadsticks in a sealed plastic bag at room temperature for up to 2 days, or freeze in a sealed freezer bag with the air pressed out for up to 2 months.

SOURDOUGH CHALLAH

My mother's family was Jewish, and this recipe is adapted from my Oma's recipe. Hers was not sourdough, but the addition of the starter is delicious. Don't worry about the braiding technique here; it is simple, and in the end, the loaf looks incredibly intricate.

Makes: 1 loaf	Prep time: 20 minutes	Cook time: 30 minutes | Rise time: Dough program, plus 2 hours

1 cup (225 to 235 g) white sourdough starter, fed, active, and at room temperature

½ cup (120 ml) milk (100°F to 110°F, or 38°C to 43°C)

¼ cup (60 ml) canola oil

¼ cup (50 g) granulated sugar

3 large eggs, at room temperature, beaten, divided

1¼ teaspoons sea salt

3½ cups (420 g) white bread flour

1½ teaspoons instant dry yeast or bread machine yeast

1 tablespoon (15 ml) water

1. Place the starter, milk, oil, sugar, 2 eggs, and sea salt in the bread machine's bucket, stirring slightly to combine. Add the flour and yeast. Program the machine for Dough and press Start.

2. When the dough cycle is complete, transfer the dough to a large bowl, forming it into a tight ball. Lightly oil the top of the dough, cover loosely with a clean kitchen cloth, and let rise until doubled, about 1 hour.

3. Transfer the dough to a lightly floured work surface and divide it into 4 equal pieces. Roll each piece into a 12-inch (30-cm) rope, tapering the ends.

4. Arrange the dough ropes in parallel lines and pinch them together at the top. Lay the rope on the far right over the rope beside it, then under the next rope, and finally over the last rope on the left.

5. Repeat this pattern with the rope furthest to the right until the loaf is braided. Pinch the end pieces together and tuck the top and bottom ends under the loaf. Transfer the loaf to a parchment-lined baking sheet.

6. In a small bowl, whisk the remaining egg and water together and brush the loaf with the mixture. Set the loaf aside for about 1 hour to rise.

7. Preheat the oven to 350°F (175°C, or gas mark 4). Bake the challah until it is golden and has an internal temperature of 200°F (93°C), 28 to 30 minutes.

8. Cool the challah and serve.

9. Store the challah in a sealed plastic bag at room temperature for up to 3 days, or freeze it in a sealed freezer bag with the air pressed out for up to 2 months.

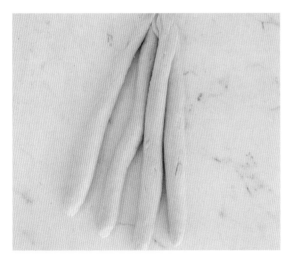

Arrange the dough ropes in parallel lines and pinch them together at the top.

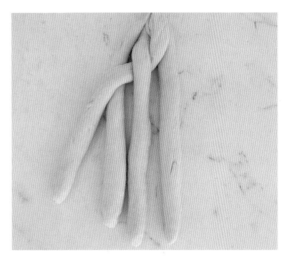

Braid the dough ropes.

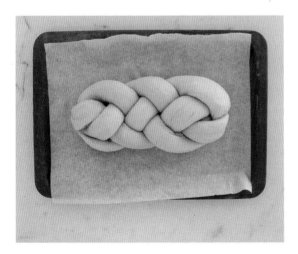

Transfer the fully braided loaf to the baking pan.

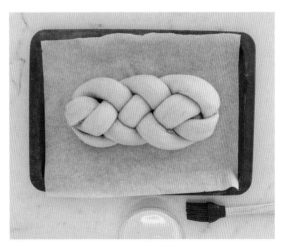

Brush the loaf with the egg-and-water mixture.

ROSEMARY SOURDOUGH FOCACCIA

Focaccia is my favorite base for flatbread pizza or when I want a delicious appetizer for friends and family. The rosemary is a traditional topping, but you can try basil, thyme, oregano, or even just a light brush of garlic oil. Serve in squares or strips with a bowl of warm marinara sauce.

Makes: 1 focaccia	Prep time: 10 minutes	Cook time: 20 minutes | Rise time: Dough program, plus 1 hour 20 minutes

1 cup (225 to 235 g) white sourdough starter, fed, active, and at room temperature

½ cup (120 ml) water (100°F to 110°F, or 38°C to 43°C)

¼ cup (60 ml) olive oil, divided

½ teaspoon sea salt

2 cups (250 g) white bread flour

1¼ teaspoons instant dry yeast or bread machine yeast

1 tablespoon (2 g) chopped fresh rosemary

1. Place the starter, water, 6 tablespoons (90 ml) of oil, and sea salt in the bread machine's bucket, stirring slightly to combine. Add the flour and yeast. Program the machine for Dough and press Start.

2. When the dough cycle is complete, transfer the dough to a large olive oil–greased bowl, turning it to coat in oil. Cover the bowl with a clean kitchen cloth and let the dough rise for 1 hour.

3. Preheat the oven to 450°F (230°C, or gas mark 8). Lightly oil a 9- x 13-inch (23- x 33-cm) baking dish.

4. Turn the dough out into the baking dish and spread it out evenly to the edges. Brush the top with the remaining 2 tablespoons (30 ml) of olive oil and sprinkle with the rosemary. Make indents all over the top with your fingertips and let the dough rise until puffy, about 20 minutes.

5. Bake the focaccia until golden brown, about 20 minutes. Cool and serve.

CHAPTER NINE

Things to Make Using Your Sourdough Discard

One of the first things you will realize when cultivating a sourdough starter is that there is lots of discard! The recipes in this chapter came about because I didn't want to waste a single delicious drop. I whipped up fluffy pancakes, decadent brownies, tender coffee cake, and cakey, chocolate-studded cookies—each bite infused with that distinctive sourdough tanginess. These recipes are now beloved family favorites, and I hope they become yours, too.

CHEESY SOURDOUGH CORNBREAD

Cornbread is a staple in most Southern kitchens in the United States, and closely guarded recipes are handed down from generation to generation to continue the tradition of this golden bread. I bet sourdough starter is the secret ingredient in many; its tangy goodness is an elusive, delicious taste that keeps people guessing. You can also add chopped jalapeño peppers, cooked bacon, or dried cranberries to this recipe to create lovely variations.

Makes: 1 loaf (8 slices)	Prep time: 10 minutes, plus 2 hours sitting time	Cook time: 40 minutes

1 cup (240 ml) whole milk

1 cup (225 to 235 g) unfed sourdough starter discard

1¼ cups (176 g) cornmeal

¾ cup (94 g) all-purpose flour

2 large eggs, at room temperature

½ cup (120 ml) melted butter, cooled

3 tablespoons (60 g) honey

2 teaspoons (9 g) baking powder

¾ teaspoon baking soda

¼ teaspoon sea salt

½ cup (58 g) shredded Cheddar

1. In a large bowl, stir the milk, starter discard, cornmeal, and flour until well combined. Cover loosely with plastic wrap and let the mixture sit at room temperature for 2 hours.

2. Preheat the oven to 350°F (175°C, or gas mark 4). Lightly spray a 9- x 5-inch (23- x 13-cm) loaf pan with nonstick cooking spray.

3. In a small bowl, mix the eggs, butter, honey, baking powder, baking soda, and sea salt. Add to the cornmeal mixture until just blended. Fold in the cheese.

4. Pour the batter into the loaf pan and bake until a toothpick inserted in the center comes out clean, 30 to 40 minutes.

5. Cool the cornbread in the pan before slicing.

6. Store the cornbread in an airtight container in the refrigerator for up to 5 days or in the freezer for up to 1 month.

SOURDOUGH SODA BREAD

Soda bread is often thought to be Irish in origin, but First Nations people where I live made this bread for hundreds of years before the Irish. Traditional versions do not contain yeast, but the addition of a sourdough starter alters the texture, so it is slightly denser and can be used for sandwiches.

Makes: 1 loaf (8 slices)	Prep time: 15 minutes	Cook time: 45 minutes

2½ cups (314 g) all-purpose flour

½ cup (48 g) rolled oats

1 tablespoon (15 g) packed brown sugar

1½ teaspoons baking powder

1 teaspoon baking soda

1 teaspoon sea salt

1 cup (225 to 235 g) unfed sourdough starter discard

¾ cup (175 ml) whole or 2 percent milk, at room temperature, plus extra for brushing

1 large egg, at room temperature, beaten

2 tablespoons (30 ml) canola oil

1. Preheat the oven to 400°F (200°C, or gas mark 6).

2. In a large bowl, combine the flour, oats, brown sugar, baking powder, baking soda, and sea salt until well combined.

3. In a medium bowl, whisk the starter discard, milk, egg, and oil until blended. Add the wet ingredients to the dry ingredients, mixing to create a sticky dough. If the dough is too sticky, add 1 tablespoon (8 g) of flour; if too dry, add more milk.

4. Turn the dough out onto a lightly floured surface and knead three or four times to bring it together.

5. Form the dough into a rough ball and place it on a parchment-lined baking sheet. Use a sharp knife to cut an "X" in the center, about ½ inch (1 cm) deep.

6. Brush the top of the dough with milk and bake until golden brown, 40 to 45 minutes.

7. Cool loaf on a rack for 20 minutes and then serve.

8. Store the bread in a sealed plastic bag at room temperature for up to 4 days, or freeze it in a sealed freezer bag with the air pressed out for up to 1 month.

SOURDOUGH BANANA BREAD

My nineteen-year-old son took one bite of this bread and proclaimed it the best he had ever tried, and I had to agree. Perfectly sweet, strong banana flavor, and a wonderfully moist texture. If you are a fan of pecans in your banana bread, add ¾ cup (83 g) after mixing up the batter.

Makes: 1 loaf (8 slices)	Prep time: 10 minutes	Cook time: 45 minutes

2 large bananas, mashed

1 cup (225 to 235 g) unfed sourdough starter discard

¾ cup (150 g) granulated sugar

½ cup (120 ml) melted butter, cooled

¼ cup (38 g) unpacked brown sugar

1 large egg, at room temperature

1 teaspoon vanilla

1½ cups (188 g) all-purpose flour

1 teaspoon baking soda

½ teaspoon sea salt

1. Preheat the oven to 350°F (175°C, or gas mark 4). Lightly grease a 9- x 5-inch (23- x 13-cm) loaf pan with butter and dust with flour.

2. In a large bowl, stir together the mashed bananas, starter discard, sugar, melted butter, brown sugar, egg, and vanilla until well mixed.

3. Add the flour, baking soda, and sea salt. Stir until just combined. Pour the batter into the prepared loaf pan and bake until well browned and a knife inserted in the center comes out clean, about 45 minutes.

4. Let the loaf cool completely on a rack and serve.

5. Store the bread in a sealed plastic bag in the refrigerator for up to 4 days, or freeze it in a sealed freezer bag with the air pressed out for up to 1 month.

CINNAMON COFFEE CAKE

Coffee cake is one of the pleasures of life, with its lightly spiced, buttery, sweet ripple through the middle and on top. I adapted a cherished family recipe to include a sourdough starter. Add one chopped apple to the batter for extra bursts of flavor.

| Makes: 9 squares | Prep time: 15 minutes | Cook time: 40 minutes |

For the Cake

½ cup (120 ml) butter, at room temperature

½ cup (115 g) packed brown sugar

½ cup (100 g) granulated sugar

2 large eggs, at room temperature

1½ teaspoons vanilla extract

2 cups (250 g) all-purpose flour

1 teaspoon baking powder

1 teaspoon baking soda

½ teaspoon sea salt

1 cup (225 to 235 g) unfed sourdough starter discard

For the Crumble

⅓ cup (75 g) packed brown sugar

⅓ cup (42 g) all-purpose flour

2 teaspoons (5 g) ground cinnamon

⅓ cup (75 g) cold butter, cut into small chunks

1. Preheat the oven to 350°F (175°C, or gas mark 4). Lightly grease a 9-inch (23-cm) square baking dish and dust with flour.

2. In a large bowl, beat the butter, brown sugar, and granulated sugar with electric hand beaters until fluffy, scraping down the sides, about 2 minutes. Beat in the eggs and vanilla until blended.

3. Using the large holes on a box grater, grate the butter into the flour mixture. In a medium bowl, stir the flour, baking powder, baking soda, and sea salt until blended.

4. Alternate adding the starter discard and the dry ingredients, half of each at a time, and mix until combined. Spoon half the batter into the baking dish.

5. In a small bowl, mix the brown sugar, flour, and cinnamon. Add the butter and rub the ingredients together until the mixture resembles coarse crumbs.

6. Sprinkle half the mixture over the batter in the baking dish, then spoon the remaining batter over the crumble. Top the batter with the remaining crumble.

7. Bake until a toothpick inserted into the center comes out clean, about 40 minutes.

8. Cool completely, then cut into 9 squares and serve.

9. Store in an airtight container in the refrigerator for up to 4 days or in the freezer for up to 1 month.

SOURDOUGH BISCUITS

Biscuits are a welcome addition to any table; there is nothing like opening up a cloth-wrapped basket of these steaming beauties. When I was a teenager, I was intimidated by the method used to make these, but imagine my surprise at the simplicity of the process.

Makes: 8 biscuits	Prep time: 15 minutes	Cook time: 12 minutes

1 cup (125 g) all-purpose flour

1¾ teaspoons baking powder

¾ teaspoon baking soda

½ teaspoon sea salt

½ cup (112 g) butter, frozen

1 cup (225 to 235 g) cold, unfed sourdough starter discard

1. Preheat the oven to 400°F (200°C, or gas mark 6).

2. In a large bowl, whisk the flour, baking powder, baking soda, and sea salt until blended.

3. Using large holes on a box grater, grate the butter into the flower mixture. Rub the butter into the dry ingredients using your fingertips until the mixture resembles coarse crumbs.

4. Add the starter discard and mix with a fork until just combined. Knead the mixture two or three times to press it together.

5. Turn the dough out onto a lightly floured surface and roll or pat it into a circle about 1 inch (2.5 cm) thick. Cut out 8 biscuits, about 2½ inches (6 cm) in diameter, re-rolling the scraps if necessary.

6. Place the biscuits on an ungreased baking sheet and bake until golden, about 12 minutes.

7. Serve warm.

8. Store in an airtight container in the refrigerator for up to 3 days or in the freezer for up to for 1 month.

SOURDOUGH PANCAKES

Pancakes are a staple in my house and a much-requested choice for dinner. I often used a box mix to save time, but I soon realized this recipe was speedy and produced a superior taste and delightful fluffy texture. You can add blueberries, chocolate chips, or a couple tablespoons of peanut butter to create beautiful variations. Serve with your favorite toppings, such as fresh fruit, maple syrup, or nut butter.

Serves 4 (3 pancakes)	Prep time: 15 minutes	Cook time: 12 minutes

1¼ cups (281 to 294 g) unfed sourdough starter discard

1 cup (240 ml) 2 percent or whole milk, at room temperature

2 large eggs, at room temperature

¼ cup (60 ml) melted butter, cooled

1½ cups (188 g) all-purpose flour

1 tablespoon (13 g) granulated sugar

1¼ teaspoons baking soda

1 teaspoon baking powder

½ teaspoon sea salt

1. In a large bowl, whisk together the starter discard, milk, eggs, and butter until blended. Whisk in the flour, sugar, baking soda, baking powder, and sea salt until smooth.

2. Heat a large skillet over medium-high heat and lightly grease with oil.

3. Working in batches, drop the batter into the skillet in ¼-cup (60-ml) measures, about four, and cook until the little bubbles on the top break, about 2 minutes. Flip the pancakes and cook the other side for 1 minute.

4. Transfer the pancakes to a plate and loosely cover with aluminum foil to keep them warm. Repeat with the remaining batter, greasing the skillet for each batch.

5. Serve hot.

6. Store leftover cooled pancakes in an airtight container in the refrigerator for up to 3 days.

SOURDOUGH BROWNIES

I once sent two pans of these brownies up to the cottage for my parents via my uncle. I didn't find out until twenty years later that he ate both pans himself and didn't regret a single bite. After tasting these treats, you might be tempted to do the same.

| Makes: 9 brownies | Prep time: 10 minutes | Cook time: 25 minutes |

¾ cup (168 g) melted butter, cooled

2 large eggs, at room temperature

1 teaspoon vanilla extract

¾ cup (65 g) unsweetened cocoa powder

¾ cup (200 g) granulated sugar

½ cup (115 g) packed brown sugar

⅛ teaspoon sea salt

1 cup (225 to 235 g) unfed sourdough starter discard

1. Preheat the oven to 350°F (175°C, or gas mark 4) and line a 9-inch (23-cm) square baking dish with parchment paper. Lightly grease the paper with melted butter.

2. In a large bowl, whisk together the melted butter, eggs, and vanilla until blended. Whisk in the cocoa powder, granulated sugar, brown sugar, and sea salt.

3. Add the starter discard and whisk until smooth. Pour the batter into the baking dish and bake until a toothpick inserted in the center has no wet batter on it (wet crumbs are fine) about 25 minutes.

4. Cool and cut into 9 brownies.

5. Store in an airtight container in the refrigerator for up to 4 days or in the freezer for up to 1 month.

SOURDOUGH BLUEBERRY MUFFINS

My husband has an obsession with blueberries, which is convenient because they grow all over where I live; you have to step over the plants when walking the dogs. When the berries are in season, I make these muffins every two weeks and freeze them for my husband's work, so I always have some on hand.

Makes: 12 muffins	Prep time: 10 minutes	Cook time: 25 minutes

1 cup (225 to 235 g) unfed sourdough starter discard

¾ cup (150 g) granulated sugar, plus extra for sprinkling

2 large eggs, at room temperature

¼ cup (60 ml) melted butter, cooled

1 teaspoon vanilla extract

2 cups (250 g) all-purpose flour

1 teaspoon baking soda

½ teaspoon sea salt

¼ teaspoon baking powder

2 cups (290 g) fresh blueberries

1. Preheat the oven to 425°F (220°C, or gas mark 7) and line a 12-cup muffin tin with liners.

2. In a large bowl, whisk the starter discard, sugar, eggs, butter, and vanilla until well blended.

3. In a medium bowl, combine the flour, baking soda, sea salt, and baking powder.

4. Add the dry ingredients to the wet and stir until just combined. Fold in the blueberries.

5. Scoop the batter evenly into the muffin cups and sprinkle with sugar. Bake until golden brown and a toothpick inserted in the center of one comes out clean, about 25 minutes.

6. Cool muffins on rack and serve.

7. Store the muffins in an airtight container in the refrigerator for up to 5 days or in the freezer for up to 1 month.

SOURDOUGH CHOCOLATE CHIP COOKIES

These are cakey-style cookies rather than crisp and flat. I often flatten them out a little extra, so they spread out more. The tangy flavor from the sourdough starter creates a complexity in the cookie, which becomes more pronounced as they cool. Try milk chocolate chips if you like a sweeter treat.

Makes: 12 cookies	Prep time: 10 minutes	Cook time: 8 minutes

¾ cup (168 g) butter, at room temperature

¾ cup (170 g) packed brown sugar

¼ cup (50 g) granulated sugar

1 cup (225 to 235 g) unfed sourdough starter discard

1 large egg, at room temperature

2 teaspoons (10 ml) vanilla extract

2 cups (250 g) all-purpose flour

1 teaspoon baking soda

½ teaspoon sea salt

2 cups (360 g) dark or semisweet chocolate chips

1. Preheat the oven to 350°F (175°C, or gas mark 4).

2. In a large bowl, cream the butter, brown sugar, and granulated sugar with electric hand beaters or a whisk until fluffy, about 2 minutes.

3. Add the starter discard, egg, and vanilla and beat until just combined, scraping down the sides with a spatula.

4. Add the flour, baking soda, and sea salt and mix with a spoon to combine. Fold in the chocolate chips.

5. Use a large spoon (about 2 tablespoons [28 g]) to drop the cookie dough onto a parchment-lined baking sheet about 1½ inches (3.5 cm) apart.

6. Bake until golden and still a little soft in the center, about 8 minutes. Let the cookies cool for 10 minutes on the baking sheet, then transfer them to a wire rack to cool completely.

7. Store the cookies in an airtight container in the refrigerator for up to 5 days or in the freezer for up to 1 month.

SOURDOUGH LEMON SCONES

This is my go-to pick-me-up treat because lemon is my favorite flavor outside of chocolate. The glaze is a must because its intense sweet-sour coating boosts the citrus taste. You can add 1 cup (145 g) of fresh blueberries for a classic dessert pairing.

Makes: 8 scones	Prep time: 15 minutes	Cook time: 25 minutes

For the Scones

2 cups (250 g) all-purpose flour

¼ cup (50 g) granulated sugar

2 teaspoons (9 g) baking powder

Zest of 1 lemon

½ teaspoon baking soda

½ teaspoon sea salt

½ cup (112 g) unsalted butter, frozen

½ cup (112 to 118 g) unfed sourdough starter discard

½ cup (120 ml) heavy cream, divided

2 teaspoons (10 ml) pure vanilla extract

For the Glaze

1 cup (120 g) confectioners' sugar

Juice of 1 lemon

1. Preheat the oven to 400°F (200°C, or gas mark 6).

2. In a large bowl, whisk the flour, sugar, baking powder, lemon zest, baking soda, and sea salt until well combined. Using the large holes on a box grater, grate the butter into the flour mixture. Use your fingers to rub until the mixture forms pea-size crumbs.

3. In a small bowl, whisk together the starter discard, ⅓ cup (80 ml) or heavy cream, and vanilla. Drizzle the mixture into the flour mixture and toss until just moistened.

4. Pour the mixture onto a lightly floured work surface and use floured hands to pat it into an 8-inch (20-cm) disc. Use a sharp knife to cut the disc into 8 equal wedges. Place the scones on a parchment-lined baking sheet.

5. Brush the scones with the remaining heavy cream and bake until lightly browned, about 25 minutes. Let cool on a rack for 10 minutes.

6. While the scones are cooling, in a small bowl, whisk the confectioners' sugar and lemon juice until blended.

7. Drizzle the glaze over the warm scones and serve.

8. Store the scones in an airtight container at room temperature for up to 2 days or in the refrigerator for up to 5 days.

SOURDOUGH PIZZA CRUST

If I had known how easy it was to make pizza dough, I would have whipped it up weekly while in university. Pizza dough is terrific for more than pizza; try it for panzerotti, turnovers, or cut into strips and baked with a sprinkle of Parmesan cheese. This dough freezes beautifully, so you can enjoy it anytime.

Makes: 3 (1-pound) dough balls	Prep time: 15 minutes	Cook time: 12 minutes Rise time: Dough program

1 cup (225 to 235 g) unfed sourdough starter discard

1¼ cups (295 ml) water (100°F to 110°F, or 38°C to 43°C)

2 tablespoons (30 ml) olive oil

1 tablespoon (13 g) granulated sugar

1¼ teaspoons sea salt

4 cups (480 g) white bread flour

1½ teaspoons instant dry yeast or bread machine yeast

1. Place the starter discard, water, oil, sugar, and sea salt in the bread machine's bucket, stirring slightly to combine. Add the flour and yeast. Program the machine for Dough and press Start.

2. When the dough cycle is complete, transfer the dough to a floured work surface. Divide it into 3 equal pieces, forming each into a ball.

3. Use the dough at this point or store it in sealed plastic bags in the freezer for up to 2 months. Thaw the dough in the refrigerator overnight before using it.

4. If baking immediately, let it rest for 20 minutes to relax the gluten. Spread a dough ball on a baking sheet or pizza pan and top with your favorite toppings. Bake in a preheated 450°F (230°C, or gas mark 8) oven until crispy and golden, about 12 minutes. Serve.

SOURDOUGH PIE CRUSTS

A foolproof pie crust recipe is cooking gold; nothing beats a flaky, golden crust for all your pie needs. This one is ideal for both savory and sweet creations because the sourdough starter balances the sugar. You can also use whole wheat flour instead of white flour.

Makes: 2 pie crusts	Prep time: 10 minutes, plus chilling time	

2 cups (250 g) all-purpose flour

1 tablespoon (13 g) granulated sugar

1 teaspoon sea salt

1 cup (225 g) unsalted butter, frozen

1 cup (225 to 235 g) unfed sourdough starter discard

1. In a large bowl, combine the flour, sugar, and sea salt until well mixed. Using the large holes on a box grater, grate the butter into the flour mixture. Use your fingers to rub until the mixture forms pea-size crumbs.

2. Add the starter discard to the flour mixture and toss until it is just combined and comes together when pressed.

3. Divide the dough into 2 equal portions and gently press each into a disc.

4. Place the discs into sealed plastic bags with the air pressed out and refrigerate for at least 2 hours before using. Or freeze in a sealed freezer bag with the air pressed out for up to 1 month. Thaw the dough in the refrigerator overnight if using from frozen.

Acknowledgments

Thank you to my tasters—my husband, Scott, and my sons, Mac and Cooper—who enthusiastically tried every loaf, sometimes before the bread cooled. Your feedback improved the recipes and boosted my confidence. I would like to thank Dan Rosenberg and the fabulous team at Quarto for their support and input.

About the Author

Michelle Anderson is the author and certified ghostwriter of over sixty books, many focused on healthy diets and delicious food. She worked as a professional chef for more than twenty-five years, honing her craft overseas in North Africa and all over Ontario, Canada, in fine dining restaurants. She worked as a corporate executive chef for RATIONAL Canada for four years, collaborating with her international counterparts and consulting in kitchens all over Southern Ontario and in the United States. Michelle ran her own catering company and personal chef business, and she was a wedding cake designer, as well. Her focus was food as medicine and using field-to-fork wholesome quality ingredients in vibrant visually impactful dishes. Michelle lives in Temiskaming Shores, Ontario, Canada, with her husband, two Newfoundland dogs, one black Lab, and three cats.

Index